D0842518

THE LEGEND OF

JESSE OWENS

Hank Nuwer

An Impact Biography
Franklin Watts
A Division of Grolier Publishing
New York London Hong Kong Sydney
Danbury, Connecticut

Acknowledgments
Grateful acknowledgment is made for research assistance provided by Robert Waite, Lisa Waite Wise, and the library staffs at the Library of Congress, Cedar Crest College, Ohio State University, Cleveland Public Library, Indianapolis Public Library, and New York Public Library.

For my sons, Christian and Adam Nuwer, nieces and nephews, and wife Jenine

Photographs ©: AP/Wide World Photos: 30, 109; Archive Photos: cover, 1 (Popperfoto), 10, 125; Corbis-Bettmann: 49, 53, 67, 74, 81, 94, 108, 110; Erik Novak: 176; Ohio State University Archives: 36, 42, 56, 69, 91, 148.

Visit Franklin Watts on the Internet at:
http://publishing.grolier.com

Library of Congress Cataloging-in-Publication Data

Nuwer, Hank.
The Legend of Jesse Owens / Hank Nuwer, 1946–
p. cm. — (An Impact biography)
Includes biographical references and index.
Summary: Explores the personal life, athletic accomplishments, and career of Jesse Owens.
ISBN: 0-531-11356-6
1. Owens, Jesse, 1913–1980—Juvenile literature. 2. Afro-American athletes—Biography—Juvenile literature. [1. Owens, Jesse, 1913–1980. 2. Track and field athletes. 3. Afro-Americans—Biography.] I. Title
GV697.09N88 1998
796.42'092
[B]—dc21   96-51188

                                                     CIP
                                                     AC

CONTENTS

Introduction

Jesse Owens discovered his gift for running track in grade school. A shy boy, his victories gave him confidence and made him feel good about his frail body. His legs were spindly but strong. He probably would have been just another fast local kid if something important hadn't occurred. In the eighth grade he learned a lesson about losing that one day would help him become the world's fastest man.

At that time, Jesse began running quarter-mile races against much older boys. He had previously defeated opponents who were his own age and younger. Now he seldom won, and he was frustrated. Jesse knew he was a faster runner than those who beat him. The losses confused him, because he had done his best. Before every race, he vowed that this would be the day he won. He made sure his opponents realized that winning meant everything to him. He glowered at them and tried to intimidate them.

Still, he continued losing. Experienced racers caught him before he could snap the ribbon at the finish line. Again and again they captured the glory that he wanted so much. Discouraged and tired of defeat, Jesse asked Charles Riley, his wise and caring track coach, for advice. Riley coached all the district teams, from elementary through junior high school. He had discovered Jesse's running abilities when the boy was in the fourth grade.

Jesse asked his coach question after question. Why

did he always fall behind and lose? What was wrong with his form? Why couldn't he seem to win?

An older man in his fifties, Riley had always looked beyond Jesse's puny physique, seeing heart, stamina, and talent in the young runner. The coach smiled. Yes, he had something to teach Jesse. He had waited until the boy asked for help, knowing that only then would the advice be heard.

The lesson was set for the following Sunday. Riley told his eager pupil that the two of them were going for a long automobile ride. "We're going to watch the best runners in the whole world," the coach said. Owens later wrote in his autobiography that Riley's words intrigued and mystified him. Who was he going to see? He wondered whether any Olympic gold medalists were going to be in northern Ohio that weekend.

On Sunday at one o'clock, Jesse scampered into the coach's car. Riley drove for hours before pulling into the parking lot of a racetrack. Jesse looked at Riley in confusion. His coach had brought him to watch *horses* race, not people. "I want you to watch these horses run," explained the coach. "No man in the world can come close to them."

Riley told Jesse to watch the winning horses' expressions and movements. "Isn't that beautiful?" Riley murmured, picking out a marvelous animal. "Look at the muscles in his neck—how easy they're resting while he gallops." The boy studied the horses in race after race as hard as he had ever studied his books. Not until the two headed back for Cleveland did Riley ask what his pupil had observed.

"Well, the way they move . . . it's like they're not trying," said Jesse. "Like it's easy. But you know they *are* trying."

The coach nodded. "And what about their faces?"

6

The young runner looked puzzled. "I didn't see anything on their faces."

Riley smiled. Jesse didn't know it, but he had given the proper response.

"Horses are honest," said Riley, his words thick with an Irish brogue. "No animal has ever tried to stare another one down. That's for actors."[1]

Jesse swallowed hard, realizing the significance of Riley's lesson even before the coach finished talking. Jesse was intelligent as well as fast.

Hoping to get a psychological edge on the other runners, Jesse had tried to stare them down. He had put his energy into showmanship when it should have gone into running. Now he knew that he had to win a victory over his own self-control before he could beat someone else.

"Do you know why the best horses make it look easy?" said Riley. "Because the determination is all on the inside where no one can see it."

Jesse settled back into his seat. The coach had given him much to think about, for the ride home and for the rest of his life. From that day on, Jesse put his emotions aside when he ran. He concentrated his energies on learning to mimic the motion of a champion racehorse—easy, but fluid and powerful.[2]

With each succeeding win on the athletic field, Jesse's self-confidence expanded. Over time, Jesse—the son of African-American parents—grew close to the small, energetic coach. Riley, of Irish descent, became a lifelong mentor—a second father, as Jesse preferred to say. Riley believed in Jesse, and that was precisely what the runner needed to bring out his best efforts. Not content with being the best runner in the Cleveland area, Jesse Owens worked and worked until he became good enough to beat any runner in the world.

Less than ten years after Coach Riley took him to the racetrack, Jesse found himself in the Olympic Games, representing the United States in four important track-and-field events. This is the story of how a once-sickly young boy became the greatest athlete of his day and, some experts would argue, of all time. But more importantly, it is the story of an American sports legend whose life and victories had more significance than the mere accumulation of awards. This is the story of a dignified athlete who overcame both his own frailties and the prejudice of white America to become a contemporary hero. Jesse Owens's fame and intercultural significance have long outlived the many world records he set.

CHAPTER 1

The Grandson of Slaves

Born in Oakville, Alabama, on September 12, 1913, James Cleveland Owens was both poor and sickly. His parents were uneducated, the children of former slaves. Because his skin was dark, his parents must have feared J. C. would be stereotyped, ridiculed, and abused by white bigots who lived in that area of the Deep South. Like many Americans, J.C. would one day learn that his ancestors came to this country on a boat. Unlike the white immigrants, his people came unwillingly. They were Africans who had been shipped to North America by slave traders. Constrained by shackles, they were among the fortunates who survived the tedious, exhausting, and dangerous voyage across the Atlantic Ocean to toil as slaves.[1]

Mary Emma and Henry Cleveland Owens, James Cleveland's parents, grew up in the sparsely populated farmlands of Oakville. Perhaps because she was older than her husband, Emma (who rarely used her first name) dominated the Owens household. Henry and Emma were sharecroppers, an existence little less backbreaking than that endured by their own parents before the Emancipation Proclamation freed them. Like many sharecroppers, both white and black, the couple worked the land of landlords, who prospered while their tenants remained poor.

J. C. was the baby of the family. Emma fondly called him her "gift child." She bore him in her late thirties when she thought that she could bear no more chil-

Jesse was born in the rural South to parents who had worked as sharecroppers. The children pictured here are picking cotton in his home state of Alabama.

dren. She had three daughters and seven sons (including J. C.) who lived. Three babies died at birth.[2]

The landlord allowed the Owenses to live in a shanty, and it was home even though dilapidated and drafty. The shack's cardboard-reinforced walls could not keep out the wind. When it rained, water leaked through the roof onto the floor and family possessions. The only heat came from the fireplace in the front room. Since his parents could not afford a hospital, it was here that J. C. Owens was born.[3]

The landlord provided everything the Owenses needed to survive, but no more than that. He took all the advantage he could of tenants who could neither read nor write. He paid them low wages and charged them exhorbitant prices for food and necessities, even charging Henry for the use of tools and machinery.

And after the crop—often cotton—was harvested, he deducted these costs from what Henry and Emma had earned.

Henry and Emma allowed J. C. to attend school, even though his absence from home meant more work for them. Schools were segregated then, so J. C. attended an all-black school taught by a volunteer teacher with weak educational credentials. The lack of a proper education in his formative years was difficult for Jesse to overcome.[4]

The Owenses mostly lived on a diet of beans and onions. They drank the same cold water that was all they had for showers, including in winter.[5] Even when Henry was 30, he owned nothing except for the mule he had inherited from his own sharecropper daddy. "Not starving was the best you could do," Jesse was to write years later in his autobiography.

Like the slaves before them, sharecroppers exhausted themselves picking cotton. It was one of the hardest agricultural jobs that any human being could undertake to do by hand. Henry harvested cotton in two ways, stooped painfully over or down on his knees, carrying a sack that weighed as much as 75 pounds (34 kilograms) when filled. Thorns on the stem made his hands bloody until they grew hard with calluses. There was no lunch wagon or rest room nearby. Henry began at dawn and came home forlorn and fatigued at dusk. Every member of the family, including young J. C., always pitched in to help. As a result, Jessie's early education was further compromised.[6]

In addition to the indignities associated with such backbreaking work, Henry was always tense when he talked to the white landlord. A black man never knew when something he did or said innocently might be wrongly construed.

Curiously, for all his athletic ability later in life,

young J. C. was not blessed with great physical gifts at birth. As a child he was susceptible to illnesses associated with weak lungs. On at least four occasions he came near death from pneumonia, his body impossibly hot to the touch with fever. His uneducated parents referred to the malady as the "devil's cold."[7]

J. C. was said by his family to be accident prone. In his autobiographical writings, he describes several mishaps, any one of which could easily have been catastrophic. He nearly severed one foot when he blundered into the jaws of a trap that Henry had set for animals. On another occasion he wandered into the path of a farm vehicle and was struck; somehow he emerged unscathed. Once he angered some local white boys, who were bent on carving their initials into his face. However, J. C.'s older brothers saved his good looks.

When he was about five years old, J. C. had another close call with death. The skin on his torso and legs developed strange growths. Unable to afford even a local doctor, let alone a skin specialist, Emma removed the growths by herself. She used a knife, although she had no anaesthesia to stop the pain. The mother, frightened but determined to do what she thought had to be done, inserted the blade into her son's chest above his heart to cut out one growth. She prayed that infection would not settle inside her boy. All she knew enough about doctoring was to sterilize the knife in a fire and to boil compresses in a kettle.

Henry feared the worst. He tried to console his wife, certain they were destined to lose another child. "If the Lord wants him—"

Emma cut him off as cleanly if he were another growth. "The Lord doesn't want this child," she said sternly.[8]

As a man, Jesse Owens remembered the terrible pain he had to endure during the operation. Fearful that he might die should he pass out, the youngster kept himself conscious throughout every slice and tear as his mother used the knife like a surgeon. "Aww, Momma, no," he heard himself screaming, his panic fueled by the torment on his father's face.

Finally, the growths came off, accompanied by bleeding that would not stop. The frantic parents used rags, towels, crop bags, and even their own clothing in an attempt to stop the relentless red flow. Weak and dazed, the patient slipped in and out off awareness, once seeing his mother's blouse soaked in his blood. Days passed and still the wounds bled. J. C. awoke in darkness to find his father praying aloud, trying to bargain with God.

"Please don't take him from me, Lord," begged Henry. "I'll do anything—the hardest thing—anything to pay you back."

Seeing J. C. stir, his father implored his son to join him in prayer. "Pray, James Cleveland," he said.

The boy asked his father what prayer to say, but Henry said he didn't know. The boy closed his eyes and prayed with words he could not recall later. Henry lifted the boy in his arms, convinced that the miraculous had occurred. J. C. bled no more.[9]

J. C. recovered. The terrible growths never returned. He gained a belief in religion after his ordeal that was to sustain him in some dark moments late in life. In spite of his frailties and accidents, young J. C. also found comfort in the fact that his condition was no worse than that of other young whites and blacks in north-central Alabama. Even though his family never had presents to put under the tree at Christmas, Henry and his older sons usually managed to find a tree that the family decorated with such odds and ends as socks and colored string.

"We used to have a lot of fun," Jesse later declared,

saying at times he felt like "the happiest kid" he knew. "We always ate. The fact that we didn't have steak—who had steak?"[10]

Children of sharecroppers seldom played with storebought toys. Their activities included tag, hide-and-seek, and running games. J. C. would "run and play like everybody else, but you never could catch him," one of those playmates, a first cousin, later told an interviewer.[11] The boy ran as though gasoline fueled him instead of flesh and blood.

J. C. was usually quiet and obedient. He did, however, possess a mischievous streak that occasionally got him into trouble. One day he had taken a knife to a bar of soap and carefully trimmed it to resemble an onion. After his unsuspected mother dumped it into a special Sunday stew she was cooking, the "onion" spewed bubbles everywhere. Needless to say, the food was ruined. J. C. received the only spanking of his life when Henry learned what his youngest had done.[12]

J. C. occasionally demonstrated that he was the family's biggest dreamer. One Sunday, when he and his family took their weekly nine-mile (almost six-kilometer) walk home from church services, the conversation got around to what everyone wanted to do when times turned better. The Owens girls said they hoped to marry men with good jobs. One brother hoped to move to the city and another said he wanted to own a piece of land. J. C.'s turn came.

"I want to go to college," he said, reminded of a time that the landlord's son had boasted the same thing.

When all the laughter died down, Henry started it up again by calling J. C. "the crazy one" of the Owenses. Emma just gave her son an affectionate squeeze. "James Cleveland Owens!" she said. "Where in the world do you get your ideas?"[13]

But Emma never mocked J. C.'s notions, because she too had a "crazy" dream of her own. She envisioned taking her whole family north to find a better life. In her dream, she saw her husband working a fine job and all her children attending high school. A church would be nearby instead of nine miles away, and she could afford to put store-bought meat on the table.

Emma had decided to turn her dreams for the family into reality. She had badgered Henry to take his share of the next crop and head north for a new and—she hoped—better life. Unknown to J. C.'s mother, she and her family were about to become part of a large movement from the South to the North that historians today call the Great Black Migration. Some 6.5 million black Americans made a similar trek to the large urban strongholds of the North, such as Chicago, Buffalo, Detroit, New York, and Cleveland. As more and more cotton began to be picked by machine, the need increased dramatically for Southern blacks to search for work.

"The black migration was one of the largest and most rapid mass internal movements of people in history—perhaps *the* greatest not caused by the immediate threat of execution or starvation," wrote historian Nicholas Lemann in *The Promised Land*. "In sheer numbers it outranks the migration of any other ethnic group—Italians or Irish or Jews or Poles—to this country. For blacks, the migration meant leaving what had always been their economic and social base in America and finding a new one."[14]

Before the migration, most blacks farmed. A few upwardly mobile individuals taught school or preached. The thousands of job vacancies in the auto industry and other assembly plant operations gave African-Americans a fourth option. They could earn a living wage if they left the country for the city.[15]

Like many African-Americans, Emma felt that

Cleveland should be their destination. Some friends had told her that this Ohio city had been a model of integration and civil rights activism. Unfortunately for Emma, public sentiment had changed for the worse when white residents perceived the flood of blacks to be a threat to their jobs and well being.

Henry's decision to move was reached on Christmas Day, 1919. Emma's announcement to the children was terse. She told J. C. and his brothers to take the mule and farm tools to the landlord. Henry previously had sold them to him for $24. The girls, she said, would help her scrub the walls and floor.[16]

"Why, Momma?" one of J. C.'s sisters asked.

"'Cause Emma Owens don't like to leave no dirty house for someone else to live in."[17]

By sundown the Owenses and their few boxes of possessions were on a train.

"Where's the train gonna take us, Momma?" J. C. demanded.

"It's gonna take us to a better life," Emma promised him. Her voice was thick as she tried to convince herself—as well as her son—that the words were true.[18]

CHAPTER 2

A Boy and His Coach

It turned out that the Owens family had waited too long to move to Cleveland. Job opportunities had all but ended for the African-Americans pouring daily into the city by train and automobile. The response of many whites to the mass arrival of blacks was unfortunate. Convinced that so many new workers presented a threat to their own jobs, many whites developed a fierce hatred for the black community. The Owenses soon learned that prejudice existed in the North as well as the South. Many businesses refused to hire blacks; many hotels and restaurants would not serve them.

Emma Owens felt uncomfortable in smoky, bustling Cleveland. Whereas she had been outgoing in Alabama, here she became a recluse, venturing outdoors only when empty food cupboards forced her to go shopping with one of her daughters. The house she had rented was in a Polish neighborhood. Although the people were friendly enough, their customs, language, and clothing made her feel as though she had moved to a foreign land.[1]

Henry Owens fared little better. He worked for a time in a steel mill, only to find his hours reduced when the economy collapsed during the late 1920s. Hampered by a loss of vision in one eye, he remained at home except for the occasional short-term job. His older sons shared his economic plight, taking odd jobs no one else wanted—such as removing manure from the city's stockyards. Some of them married and, with no place else to go, moved in with their parents, stealing the privacy of all.[2]

J. C. alone prospered in Cleveland. All his life he would display a knack for adapting to new situations and locales. Of all Henry and Emma's children, only he would stay in school and earn a high school diploma. He had little trouble finding part-time work and his earnings helped his parents meet the rent and buy food. His biggest problem was that the principal of his new elementary school did not feel schooling in Alabama was on a par with an education in Ohio. Consequently, J. C. had to repeat the second grade with students two and three years younger than himself.[3]

J. C. was given a new first name by the Cleveland school system. On his first day at Bolton Elementary School, his teacher looked down at the timid youngster and asked for his name.

"J. C., ma'am," came the reply.

Unused to an Alabama drawl, she repeated his name wrong. "Jesse?"

"Yes, ma'am," he said, unwilling to correct a teacher. "Jesse Owens."

Jesse also received his introduction into athletic competition at Bolton Elementary. Later, he credited his success to the mentoring he received from track coach Charles Riley, who spotted his talent almost immediately.

Emma, however, nearly quashed Jesse's track career before it began. Because her youngest son had a chronic cough and looked frail, she tended to be overprotective, fearful when he tried new activities. So, when Jesse ran home from school to tell her that Charles Riley had offered to coach him, she bristled.

"I don't like it, J. C.," said Emma, unwilling to address her son by his new name. "You might get hurt."[4]

Another boy might have backed down, but Jesse

Owens was determined to run track. When he couldn't budge his mother, he begged his father to overrule her.

Henry refused, unwilling to contradict his wife. Jesse began to despair, but he tried one final argument. Athletics might help him overcome his weak constitution and build a stronger body. That's what Coach Riley had said. "I want to grow up to be strong, and be a runner like you were," said Jesse.

Henry gave his son a long look, perhaps seeing his own muscular frame superimposed on Jesse's frail body. Back home in Alabama, Henry had enjoyed showing off for his family by winning spirited footraces on Sunday afternoons against his neighbors. Jesse had loved watching his father hit full stride, legs pumping while all the other runners fell behind. But the move to the North had drained Henry's ambition. He had even told his impressionable son that "it don't do a colored man no good to get himself too high, 'cause it's a [long] drop back to the bottom," Owens recalled in his autobiography. The best Jesse could extract was a promise from his father that he would think about the issue overnight.

The next morning, to Jesse's delight, Emma said he could let Charles Riley coach him. "J. C., I don't know what's got into your father, but he wants to let you do this running," she said. "You be careful, though. You're not built like your father."

Jesse couldn't wait to tell his coach. When he did, Riley told him to stay after school, and they would get started that day. The boy's face fell. He said that his family needed the money he earned after school working, by turns, at a greenhouse and a gas station.

The coach decided to make an exception for the scrawny youngster. "If you run as hard as you work, I'll have a champion on my hands," said Riley. "Well, it looks as if the only time is *before* school. If you'll get here forty-five minutes early, so will I."[5]

19

In a few months, the hard work of the coach and runner began to bear results. One day the coach timed the boy with a stopwatch. The result so amazed him that he took the watch to a jeweler to be repaired. The watch was fine. It was Jesse's time that was out of the ordinary.[6]

Jesse grew stronger by the day. Riley knew the boy's true ability lay in short sprints, but he had him run much longer races to build his wind and endurance. The coach also taught him the valuable lesson that athletes need to think like champions before they could run like them. Winners never give anything less than their best in every race, no matter how inconsequential a meet might seem.

Jesse didn't win every race, because he was far from developed, but he did win many races. His coughing fits became fewer and finally ceased. One day the boy persuaded his mother to watch him race. Inspired by her presence, he won by several lengths.

Coach Riley took Emma aside. He told her a secret he did not yet want to tell Jesse. "I know this will shock you," he said, "but Jesse could become an Olympic champion."[7]

Emma's response has been lost over time, but perhaps she wasn't as shocked as Coach Riley had thought she would be. Ever since Jesse was little, she had told him over and over in her simple way: "What you put in is exactly what you get out."[8]

In retrospect, Riley's optimism was also shocking. Only a handful of black athletes had represented their country since the modern Olympic Games had been created by Baron Pierre de Coubertin in 1896. When Coubertin first proposed an Olympics that would include all nations, many people ridiculed him.

Coubertin proposed the idea during a formal sports assembly held at the Sorbonne in Paris. "We'll have Negroes and Chinese and—and—redskins!" one heckler shouted derisively. The Sorbonne dissolved in laughter. The idea of Indians and athletes with yellow and black skin competing seemed too absurd for their racist minds to comprehend.[9]

Ignoring the odds against them, Riley and his young athlete continued to work together year after year. The coach continued entering Jesse in the 220-yard event, holding him back from the shorter sprints until he thought the runner had learned all he could and strengthened his weak lungs.

Jesse had progressed to the point where he now gave every race his complete concentration. He no longer made faces at the other runners to try to intimidate them. He ran his own race and let them run theirs. But he still had much to learn about proper running techniques and the secrets of running that can be learned only with experience.

Good form meant everything, Coach Riley taught him. Don't look to either side to catch a glimpse of your opponents. Always keep your chin straight. Riley even showed his athletes how to walk properly, swinging their arms in an athletic manner. He reminded them that success was never achieved in a day, half-seriously telling them to train for an imaginary race to be held "four years from Friday."[10]

"Don't worry about running fast," Riley told him over and over. "Just run *right*. The speed will come by itself."[11]

Jesse also learned that the length of a race put special demands on a runner. He had much to learn about pacing himself. Determined to give his best, he ran the 220-yard dash with the same all-out effort he gave the 100-yard dash. As a result, in one important junior high school race, Jesse built a tremendous lead, only to have two opponents nip him at the finish line.

Disgusted with his third-place finish, Jesse refused

to stop running until he came up against a brick wall flanking the track. He hit it hard, bruising an elbow, and was gasping in pain, disbelief and frustration when Coach Riley came hurrying to his side.

"Congratulations, Jesse," said Riley. "You won today. Even when the race was over, you didn't stop."

The distraught boy looked at him, realizing his coach was sincere, not mocking him. By not letting up, the runner had shown his coach that he was building character. Technique can be learned, his coach had taught him, but an athlete—just like any other human being—either possesses character or he does not.

The coach, usually a man of few words, was not finished. "Tomorrow's a new day, and because you beat your opponent today doesn't mean that you'll beat him tomorrow," he said. "But if you do beat him again tomorrow, and again next week, and again next year, and you keep on winning over him, you'll go to the Olympics someday."[12]

Charles Riley continued to be Jesse's coach after the boy graduated from Bolton and registered at Fairmount Junior High School. His guidance cannot be overestimated, particularly since Henry Owens was unemployed and ceased to exercise much influence over his youngest son.

"I grew to admire and respect [Riley's] words and actions and everything else," Jesse once said. "I wanted to be like him because he was a wonderful person, well-liked by everybody, no problems with anybody, and he preferred working over there with those Negro kids rather than going into . . . a white area."[13]

The coach, in turn, came to look upon Jesse as a son, even encouraging the boy to call him "Pop." He himself had two sons, but neither had athletic ability. Jesse frequently ate at the Riley home, learning table manners from the coach's wife. The coach also stressed

22

that few people go through life without trials. Jesse needed to respond to life's challenges with grace and courage.[14]

"The good Lord has given you a special talent, Jesse," the coach reminded him. "But never forget this: There's bound to come a time in your life when you'll be asked for more than ability."[15]

Riley used colorful expressions to get his point across, and Jesse never forgot them. "Run like you're on a red-hot stove," the coach said again and again. "You don't ever want your feet to even touch it. But they have to, don't they? Okay, then, take those feet off that red-hot stove just as soon as you set them down on it."[16]

With every success, the ambitions of both the coach and the athlete grew. Jesse was determined to forge a better life for himself. He had only to look to the examples of his father and brothers to know that life could be cruel to those who failed to achieve. But Jesse did not run just to prove something to himself and Charles Riley. He also ran because it was fun. He knew a pure kind of joy when he was on a track, putting every ounce of his energy into beating his best time on the coach's omnipresent stopwatch. The greatest day of his young life came on an occasion when his coach timed him in the 100-yard dash.

After carefully going over the course to make sure that it was not a yard less than 100 yards, Riley showed his stopwatch to the proud 15-year-old. Jesse saw that it read 11 seconds flat.

"My boy," said Riley, the proud mentor. "You have tied the world [schoolboy] record."[17]

As Jesse progressed, his coach introduced him to other track-and-field events. In amazement, Riley saw that the boy showed the same aptitude for jumping that he had demonstrated in running events. Through hard work and practice, Jesse also established junior-high school records with a 6-foot high jump and a long jump of 22 feet, 11¾ inches.[18]

In addition to Coach Riley, young Jesse had another adult model in junior high school, though he met the man for only a few minutes. That man was Charley Paddock, winner of the gold medal for the 100-meter in the 1920 Olympics, and a former sprinting star at the University of Southern California. Paddock also had competed in the 1924 Olympics, earning a second-place finish in the 100-meter dash.

In 1928, Paddock visited Cleveland on a lecture tour. Coach Riley invited the Olympian to the junior high school, and later asked him to speak a few words in private with Jesse. The visit was a monumental event in the boy's life, giving him not only an idol to emulate but also an image of how a champion walks, talks, and acts.[19]

But no matter how many dreams filled Jesse's teenage head, little could he know that millions of young people one day would consider *him* to be *their* hero.

The 1936 Olympic Games were eight years away.

CHAPTER 3

Facing the Competition

Besides Charley Paddock, a white man, another role model of Jesse's was an African-American. Jesse had learned in school about the courageous Booker T. Washington. As president of the Tuskegee Institute in Jesse's native Alabama, Washington had spent his life urging American blacks to better themselves through education and mastery in business or crafts.[1]

Washington, like Jesse's grandparents, had himself been a slave. After the Civil War, he became the most famous African-American in the United States, revered for his untiring efforts to provide better lives for blacks. Because he believed that self-help was the best course of action for blacks to take, he ran into opposition from black leaders such as W. E. B. Du Bois of the National Association for the Advancement of Colored People (NAACP). Du Bois recommended that blacks move toward more militant confrontations with white America to achieve equal rights under the law.

Significantly, as an adult, Jesse Owens would later face the same kind of criticism Washington received from hardline black leaders, because of Jesse's non-militant, moderate stance on civil rights issues. Like Washington, Jesse believed that black advancement could occur only when economic parity with whites had been achieved. Washington preached that hating the white man was self-destructive. "It did not do him any harm, and it certainly was narrowing up my soul and making me a good bit less of a human being," Washington said.[2]

The educator's philosophies impressed young Jesse. "I know that the name of Booker T. Washington will live forever in the memories of the colored people," he once told a group of his own admirers. "I would like to become a little bit like him."[3]

Although Jesse's diligence in junior high school sometimes drew the scorn and envy of less committed peers who labeled him a "teacher's pet," he was determined to be a leader outside the athletic field as well as on it. Although some subjects were difficult for him, and he was handicapped by a stuttering problem, he worked hard to achieve passing grades. Fellow students recognized his efforts by electing him student council leader. His teachers rewarded his leadership by appointing him a school monitor. And Coach Riley honored him by naming him captain of the track team.[4]

In the fall of 1930, Jesse entered East Technical High School, then a trade school with a low proportion of blacks in the student body. His family continued to struggle. Furthering hampering his attempts to find steady work, Henry had fractured a leg when he accidentally stepped in front of a taxi. Emma, having grown accustomed to Cleveland, moved into the role of family breadwinner, taking in laundry to keep the rent paid, the family fed, and her youngest child in school. In 1929, the Great Depression rocked Cleveland, and many teenagers had to quit school to take whatever jobs they could find to help support their families. Emma, however, was willing to take all domestic odd jobs available to give her youngest son a chance to earn his high school diploma. None of Jesse's brothers and sisters would graduate.[5]

In retrospect, Jesse's choice to attend East Tech was unwise, made because the technical school was located a few blocks from his home. Had Jesse attended a more academically oriented high school, he almost certainly would have acquired study skills and knowledge that would have better served him in college. He would later admit that his teachers never required him to read books or challenged his mind. Students like Jesse who wished to go to college needed the structured academic environment of a more traditional high school, or— like Jesse's classmate and best friend, David Albritton— had to be exceptionally motivated to study.[6]

Jesse had felt a certain sadness upon leaving junior high school. He realized that he no longer would be under the guidance of Charles Riley. He learned that his new coach, Edgar Weil, was not only a recent college graduate and new to the job, but that his interest and expertise was in football, not track.

Weil, however, realized his own deficiencies in trying to train a potential Olympian sprinter. The coach contacted Riley, offering him a position as an assistant. Jesse's aging mentor eagerly accepted the opportunity to again work with his star pupil. Had he refused, the Olympics might have remained an unfulfilled dream for Jesse Owens.

In addition to track, Jesse tried out for football, but neither his heart nor talent was in that sport. He lasted but one week. One year he also decided to give basketball a try, but suffered an injury to his ankle. Even the school's principal counseled Jesse to stick to track, lest he damage his magnificent legs and become unfit for sprinting.[7]

In track, his first love, Jesse continued to blossom under the stern and patient Charles Riley. He became the best sprinter in the district, and he was improving rapidly in the long jump as well. East Tech had another bonafide star in David Albritton. Coach Riley believed Albritton had the potential to become a world-class high jumper. Jesse and his best friend David fantasized that someday the two of them would wear the colors of the United States in the Olympics.[8]

It was perhaps fated that Jesse and Albritton would become lifelong friends. Like Henry Owens, Albritton's father had migrated from Alabama to Cleveland, hoping that industry might be preferable to sharecropping as a way of life. The two were nearly the same age, Jesse the older by five months. The Albritton home in Alabama was only six miles from Jesse's—although the two never met as children—giving them a common culture.[9]

Another special friend was Minnie Ruth Solomon, a slender, beautiful girl who preferred to be called Ruth. She wore her hair in curls tight against her head and was considered more sensitive and mature than other girls in her crowd. The two met on Cleveland's East Side when they were preteens, sharing Ruth's umbrella in a downpour. She attended Fairmount Junior High with Jesse and was two years younger than he. Their mutual crush deepened day by day. In the accepted courting ritual of the day, Jesse occasionally carried Ruth's books and slipped her secretive messages that made her giggle.[10]

Jesse's athletic exploits must have captivated the impressionable Ruth. As he grew into maturity, his once-skinny frame developed the stout legs of his father. He now displayed sturdy and powerful muscles that his skimpy track suit emphasized. With each new victory on the track, his confidence soared. Sprinters from rival schools were awed by his polish and ability, and the *Cleveland Gazette* covered his successes.

In 1932, going into his senior year at Tech, it seemed as if Jesse's Olympic dream was going to be fulfilled. He traveled to Evanston, Illinois, to the campus of Northwestern University to try out for the U.S. Olympic team. There was more publicity for the Games than usual in American newspapers since they were going to be played in Los Angeles. Newspapers devoted to black readers also paid close attention to the Olympic trials. For the first time, it seemed possible that a significant number of black athletes might make the U.S. team. Jesse prayed that he would be one of the chosen few.

But the dream was not yet ready to come true. Destiny had another scenario in mind for Jesse Owens. The setback, seen in perspective years later, was not so very bad for Jesse. But at the time, he was crushed, his confidence shaken.

Like many young athletes, Jesse forgot to relax under pressure. The magnificent athletes drawn from all over the Midwest far surpassed the competition he had beaten in Cleveland. In particular, he felt daunted by a sprinter from Marquette University named Ralph Metcalfe, who was older, savvier, broader, and taller than Jesse. Metcalfe had already set several sprint records. His sophistication also intimidated Jesse.

Jesse competed in three events: the long jump and 100-meter and 200-meter sprints. He lost all three. Metcalfe defeated him in both short races, winning the right to compete in the U.S. Olympic team finals. Jesse's one consolation was that by the end of the trials, he and Metcalfe had formed a friendship that would never dissolve. After Jesse had lost a sprint race, he extended a hand to Metcalfe.

"I thought I *had* you," said Jesse, fighting to regain his wind.

"Maybe that's what beat you, Jesse," Metcalfe said with an enigmatic smile.

Jesse later said that it took him thirty-five years for the meaning of that remark to come clear to him. "The minute you think you've got it beaten, *you're* beaten," Jesse said Metcalfe was trying to tell him. "No matter

29

Jesse's rival Ralph Metcalfe (far right) won this 100-meter heat in Princeton, New Jersey.

what you did yesterday, each sunrise wipes the slate clean."[11]

Although Jesse never made excuses, there was another likely reason for his subpar performances. Ruth had informed him that she was pregnant with his child. Poor and still several courses away from achieving her high school diploma, she had made the decision to quit school to bear Jesse's first daughter.

Gloria Shirley arrived on August 8, 1932. The father was eighteen years old, the mother sixteen. It was probably not until 1935 that Jesse and Ruth married. Jesse later in life lied about the marriage date. Although he never could produce a marriage certificate, he claimed to have eloped with Ruth in July 1932, hoping to protect little Gloria from the stigma of illegitimacy. Society then had little tolerance for the mistakes made by teenagers. Jesse's fanciful story of an elopement was the first of several times that he would invent events in his life to protect an idealized image of himself. Some biographers have objected to the way Jesse tried to put the best light on a bad situation, but Jesse had likely concluded that the baby was his business and Ruth's, not the public's.[12]

There was no question that Jesse and Ruth were in love. "By the time I was sixteen, I realized that Ruth was the girl for me," he once said. "She said I was the one she wanted to spend the rest of her life with, too. . . . She understood what running—*what being the best at something*—meant to me."[13]

If marriage had to wait, Ruth decided that she would be patient. She knew that Jesse was determined to try out for the Olympics in 1936. She remained at home with her parents, paying for diapers and baby food with the small salary she earned working at a beauty parlor.

The distraction of Ruth's unplanned pregnancy might have thrown Jesse off course in the Olympic trials, but he managed to put his personal problems behind him for his senior year. One of the most popular students at East Tech, he won an election for student council president, no small feat at a predominantly white high school.[14]

Jesse overcame a knee injury during his senior year and enjoyed an undefeated track season. He heeded the advice of Charles Riley every time out, showing no emotion before and during a race. Only his wide smile after every victory betrayed his pleasure in winning.

Jesse attracted a following of passionate fans who intimidated rival runners and jumpers with the ferocity of their cheering. His personal magnetism won him devotees everywhere he competed. He rewrote the high school record book for the long jump and both the 100- and 200-yard sprints. With a long jump of 24 feet 3⅙ inches, he became the schoolboy champion of the world, shattering the existing record by a fraction over 3 inches.[15]

Jesse's heroics, however, were far from over. In June 1933 he traveled to the University of Chicago, competing at the National Interscholastic Meet, only a few miles south of the site of his failure at the Olympic Trials. This time, however, he was mentally and physically ready for the challenge. He broke the old world record for the 220-yard dash, finishing in 20.7 seconds. He tied the world record in the 100-yard dash with a time of 9.4 seconds. If that wasn't enough, he added a long jump of 24 feet 9⅝ inches as well. He scored 30 of East Tech's 54 points to give Coaches Riley and Weil a farewell present: first place in the most prestigious high-school meet in the Midwest.

When the team returned to Cleveland, the city's mayor, Ray Miller, threw a victory parade. Jesse and his parents were in the first convertible, waving to the cheering crowds.

When the parade was over, Jesse found himself busier than ever. It was time to select a college. Once again he hopped into Coach Riley's Model T, this time to take a tour of the University of Michigan campus. Riley strongly urged Jesse to accept an offer from Michigan, but for perhaps the first time in his life, Jesse disregarded the advice. He decided to move from Cleveland to Columbus, Ohio, where he had been accepted as a student by Ohio State University.

The move was highly unpopular with the black press, which pointed out that Ohio State's record on race relations was one of the worst in the Big Ten. The school had refused to allow two young black women to share campus housing with white women. Just how far the entire state had yet to progress in civil rights became clear when Ohio's Supreme Court upheld the university's right to discriminate against the two blacks.[16]

Even when a black newspaper turned on him for helping "advertise an institution that majors in prejudice," Jesse showed incredible spunk for a high school student by sticking to his decision. After all, he had attended a predominantly white high school and had become its most popular student. He had learned that his combination of athletic ability and personality easily won him friends. Why shouldn't the same thing happen at Ohio State?

The Ohio State Buckeyes were glad to have Jesse. "Every coach in the Big Ten . . . wanted him, but somehow he got it fixed in his head that a boy who lived in the state of Ohio should go to Ohio State," his college track coach, Larry Snyder, would later say.[17]

The decision might not have been that complicated and was made because Ohio State was willing to bend rules. Scholarships were not available then and Jesse needed money. An Ohio State alumnus promised Jesse a job as an elevator operator in a state government building in Columbus. Also, his best friend, David Albritton, had decided to run track at Ohio State. Finally, Jesse's high school academic average was only 74, and he was a few credits short of a degree. Had he decided to attend another university he might have had to return to East Tech in the fall—as David Albritton did—to get his last few credits. Instead, Ohio State allowed him to take examinations, waiving the normal requirements. In effect the school lowered its standards to land a superior athlete, and it certainly would have been unable to use such recruiting methods under today's tightened National Collegiate Athletic Association (NCAA) regulations, according to biographer William J. Baker.

As he had as a boy, Jesse told proud Emma and disbelieving Henry that he was going to college. This time, however, in the fall semester of 1933, the dream of a sharecropper's son had become reality. He was one of a mere 100 black Americans to attend Ohio State as the entire country reeled from the harsh economic effects of the Great Depression.[18]

CHAPTER 4

Living with Discrimination

Jesse's introduction to Ohio State must have disappointed and frightened him. Although he was a highly recruited athlete, he could not escape the discrimination facing African-Americans attending the school. Like the women students who had been denied university housing at Ohio State, he was not allowed to live in the school's lone male dormitory. Instead, he had to live in a boarding house in a black section of Columbus, cooking his own meals since many local restaurants were for whites only. In another form of discrimination, the elevator he ran in the Statehouse turned out to be a freight elevator; only white athletes were permitted to operate passenger elevators.

In addition to discrimination, Jesse was under pressure because his grades were low. His inadequate scholastic background and poor study habits plagued him his first two quarters, and he stood in danger of flunking out of school. All Ohio State classes were unusually large during the Depression because student-faculty ratios had been increased to save the school money. Without benefit of individual attention, he was at a disadvantage. His cultural background growing up in the rural Deep South was unlike that of most of his peers.[1]

Athletes at that time lacked the advantages enjoyed by today's collegiate track-and-field stars. College athletes now accept no jobs during their sports seasons under guidelines established by the NCAA. They are as-

Jesse chose to attend Ohio State University. He is pictured here (bottom row, second from left) along with the rest of the OSU track team.

signed academic counselors, advisors, and tutors. Study halls are provided. Athletes with full scholarships get tuition, books, and room and board.

Jesse, in contrast, worked the equivalent of a full-time job even while competing in track. Nervous and high-strung in personality, he actually preferred working to studying, hating the inactivity. He worked six days a week at three different jobs. He waited on tables in a dining room for whites. He performed various duties in the school library. He ran the freight elevator seven hours a night, trudging back to his room well past midnight. Incidentally, he found himself better off financially than he had been at any time of his life. In retrospect, he certainly would have performed better academically had he not taken all those jobs, but his financial independence must have boosted his self-esteem.[2]

Thus, Jesse never managed to get on track in his studies. He had enrolled in the physical education department, taking the easiest courses to keep eligible, but still his grades were poor. His most successful course was a class in phonetics from someone Jesse later termed "a master teacher." The instructor cured Jesse of his lifelong problem with stuttering and taught him to emulate those who spoke well. Jesse began giving speeches in Columbus elementary schools.

"I've admired the great orators . . . even more than the great athletes," Jesse revealed years later, citing Martin Luther King, Jr., New York political leader Adam Clayton Powell, and Republican Party leader Roscoe Conkling Simmons as particular inspirations. "When I was young, I used to go to banquets just to watch the mannerisms and the style of public speakers."[3]

Like his speaking talents, Jesse's athletic career also blossomed. At Ohio State, track coach Larry Snyder taught him techniques that added inches to his long jump and lopped fractions of a second from his sprint time.

"I have coached a few boys who were very, very good, but who were not easy to coach," Snyder told *Scholastic Coach* magazine in 1936. "They thought they knew how to do things, and did not want to change, and the work had to be done in a roundabout manner with them; then when the idea came to them as their idea, it was good. [In contrast,] Jesse Owens listens and then he tries to put the suggestions into practice. He is so well coordinated that even a radical 'form' change in starting, or any other phase of running, becomes a part of his style after a very few practice sessions."[4]

In two years, through hard work and determination, Snyder helped Jesse become all he could be—the world's greatest athlete. Pop Riley had taken the athlete to the limit of his coaching abilities, but Jesse still needed improvement to beat the world's best runners. This lesson was hammered home during Jesse's freshman year at Ohio State. Competing in a tournament in New York City, once again he lost to his rival at the 1932 Olympic trials—Ralph Metcalfe.

Little by little, Jesse learned from experience to get an edge over his foes. First he learned to move his arms in synchronization with his legs while sprinting. Then Jesse had to get rid of a bad habit. Rather than move explosively with the starter's command, he had started when the other runners started. Invariably, he lost precious yards at the very start of the race. While Jesse's natural speed enabled him to catch most rivals, he could not afford to give away this advantage at the start to world-class athletes like Metcalfe and still expect to win. Soon Jesse learned to start so quickly that Snyder timed him at 6.1 and 6.6 in the 60-yard and 60-meter dashes, both world records.

Jesse also learned to watch the starter's eyes, looking for a telltale sign that would indicate the precise moment when the gun would fire. He learned to explode out of the blocks, to gain position in as few strides as possible, and to "really bear down and see what you're made of"—to use his own words—during the last half of a race.[5]

Snyder found Jesse to be not only coachable but a team player. The coach sometimes had to stop him from making "one more practice run," because the athlete truly loved exerting himself. No matter how tired Jesse might be, he always volunteered to enter additional events. If the team found itself 5 points down near the end of a meet, Jesse "was willing and able to go out and get them," said Snyder. Before long, Jesse had added the low hurdles and the mile relay team to his long list of specialties.[6]

Snyder taught Jesse how to lengthen his stride and

kick powerfully while in the air to improve his long jump. Day after day, the athlete practiced fundamentals, performing a certain hopping exercise that added more than a foot to his best long jump. Nonetheless, Jesse's form in this event remained somewhat unorthodox, but Snyder decided not to tamper with that.[7]

As with the long jump, Jesse's form in the low hurdles didn't come naturally to him, but his perseverance overcame all deficiencies. He never learned how to skim a hurdle without actually touching it. One major problem was that his legs were comparatively short. Champion hurdlers have a graceful, long stride, but his short legs gave him a stride that was only seven feet. He worked hard on Thursday and Friday afternoons to overcome a tendency to bang into the first hurdle on the course instead of clearing it. If he could get by the first hurdle, he rarely had any trouble with the remaining hurdles, having attained full stride. Larry Snyder got Jesse to compensate for his shorter stride by staying in the air longer than hurdlers traditionally did. Thus, while world-class hurdlers came so close to the hurdles that they nearly touched them, Jesse left plenty of air between them and his body.[8]

Jesse's improvement became evident at the end of his first year. Competing against other freshman athletes during a Big Ten conference meet at Ohio State, he established three freshman track records. He ran the 100-yard dash in 9.6 seconds and the 220-yard run in 21 seconds flat. Officials measured his long jump at 24 feet 10 inches.

During the summer between his freshman and sophomore years, Jesse got back his old high school job as an attendant at a filling station. With money in his pockets, he and Ruth talked about getting married. At one point, he even filled out forms for a marriage license.

But while he was as mature an athlete as ever ran track, in other ways he was immature. While the loving Ruth waited patiently for him, he enjoyed the attention of young women who clustered around the service station to flirt with him. Jesse told Ruth that she was the only woman for him, but that the time was not yet right to wed. He left Cleveland to return to Columbus for his sophomore year without buying a wedding ring.[9]

Jesse put his summer earnings into a car. He and Ohio State teammate Dave Albritton purchased a rattletrap 1914 Ford that the two drove everywhere.

Since this era was long before athletic departments chartered planes to get to competitions, Jesse and his Buckeye teammates logged thousands of miles on midwestern roads. According to Jesse's recollections, while all athletes had to ride in cars, there was an important distinction. The whites rode together in the better automobiles; the blacks rode together—in clunkers. On the road, public restaurants often refused to serve the black athletes but catered to their white teammates. Even in the supposedly liberal North, sometimes blacks and whites could not shower together in gym locker rooms or stay in the same motels. The limit of Ohio State's "forward thinking" was that the administration allowed blacks to play on the same athletic teams with whites. It rarely, if ever, stood up for the civil rights of African-Americans.

Jesse was disturbed by the ill treatment that he and other blacks received. It hurt him when white teammates failed to protest when Jesse was denied a meal or forced to ride in freight elevators while they rode in passenger elevators. It just didn't occur to many of Jesse's white friends that they had a responsibility to stand up and shout when they witnessed racial injustice.[10]

"I . . . remember riding in the Ford that day and not being able to keep down the bitterness that all the Negroes had to be in one car," Owens later said in his memoirs. "At the university all the Negroes lived together in one old house. But was *that* natural?"[11]

Following the example of Booker T. Washington, his hero, Jesse elected to be a peacemaker instead of a rabble-rouser. Once, after teammates brought plates of food from a "whites-only" restaurant for the black athletes to eat inside the Ford, the angry restaurant owner snatched away the plates, affronted that blacks were eating off them. Eggs flew everywhere, staining the black athletes' clothing as well as the tattered upholstery of the car. Jesse was upset but kept cool and even put a bearlock on David Albritton to keep him from pummeling the bigot.

"[We can] never fight back," Albritton shouted in frustration.

"We *are* fighting," Jesse said. He insisted that as blacks gained greater and greater recognition in sports and other endeavors, not even the most racist restaurants owners would dare refuse to serve people of color. Those were Jesse's principles—in the tradition established by Booker T. Washington—and he was later to defend them against militant blacks who thought him too moderate.[12]

Larry Snyder counseled Jesse to show intelligence in the face of ignorance, patience in the face of intolerance, and stoicism in the face of racist rage. The coach emphasized that Jesse's athletic success put him under a microscope, and that his actions would reflect credit or shame not only on himself, but on Ohio State and the African-American race as well. As unfair as this seems in today's context, Jesse later said that his coach's advice had helped him. "Everybody's eyes were upon you," said Jesse. "And they would scrutinize everything you did, and so you had to be very careful of the things that you did."[13]

In some ways, this incredible forbearance came nat-

Larry Snyder (right) coached Jesse in college and proved to influence him both on and off the track.

urally to the athlete. Jesse had been reared a Christian by his parents, and so had been taught to turn the other cheek when facing discrimination. Charles Riley also had taught him to control his anger, teaching him that the best athletes all knew how to master their emotions.

"An angry athlete is an athlete who will lose every time, Jesse," said Riley. "You must go in there mad—but [you must cultivate] a special kind of *icy* mad where you are completely in control of your anger. Never let it control you. Once you do that, even for a split second, you may never be in control again until the event is over."[14]

As early as 1935, reporters marveled at Jesse's popularity. During a successful Western Amateur Athletic Union (AAU) meet in San Diego, California, Jesse outsprinted and outjumped Olympic hopeful Eulace Peacock. Jesse won so many friends that police had to steer him through throngs of admirers. Crowds mobbed him. Fans wanted to shake his hand, talk with him, and get his autograph.[15]

Although Jesse was polite and always willing to accommodate autograph seekers, a part of him reasoned that he had won a victory for himself and all African-Americans because some of the requests surely came from people who otherwise had a low opinion of black people. Years later, he would say that even when people were nice to him, he always wondered if some of them harbored racist thoughts in their hearts, because of how badly he'd been treated before he became famous.

"[Racism] can be pure hell at times and can shake anyone's sureness," he said. "Often it's worse if you were the world's fastest human. When you walk into [a fine establishment] wearing a face almost everyone recognizes and still feel that agonizing fear reflex deep in your gut, you still can't help wondering with a part of your soul whether the maître d's smile is a sneer and if the woman at the next table thinks you should be waiting on her instead of sitting next to her. It's worse than if you were simply an anonymous black man."[16]

Thus, though he might be angry or hurting on the inside, Jesse turned a blind public eye to discrimination, especially if he felt that a white person had offended him out of ignorance rather than malice. Sometimes he felt the digs were made by shortsighted but otherwise good people. Many journalists patronized him, calling him "a credit to his race." Papers such as the *Chicago Tribune* always made race an issue, invariably pointing out early in Jesse's career that a "colored" man had won a race. Sportswriters frequently referred to his color in the nicknames they gave him such as the "Dark Streak," "Tan Thunderbolt," and "Brown Bombshell."

Jesse preferred that the writers call him "The Buckeye Bullet." That name made reference to his school and speed, not to his race.

CHAPTER 5

The Buckeye Bullet

By 1935, Jesse had become a big man, not only on the Ohio State campus, but throughout the Big Ten. Larry Snyder had a flair for promoting his star athlete. Snyder specialized in having Jesse perform offbeat feats such as doing the 100-yard dash with a running start, clocking him at 8.4 seconds. The feat titillated the American public and, strangely enough, put him into the Sunday comics of every major newspaper in America. Jesse's time was noted in a syndicated strip called Ripley's *Believe It or Not*.[1]

In retrospect, the stunts were tawdry and undignified, although Jesse was following the fashion of the times by participating in them, as many white athletes did. Had he stuck to running and jumping events, his press clippings would have been extensive enough to make him a national legend. His most stunning performance came in 1935, when in a single day, Jesse's face, race, and name became known from one coast to another and beyond the oceans during a Big Ten Conference championship meet. On May 25, in front of some 12,000 fans filling wooden bleachers at the University of Michigan in Ann Arbor, the sophomore enjoyed what some experts have called the greatest all-time, one-person performance in track-and-field.

Many fans present were Wolverine diehards, hoping to see a Michigan triumph. Some, however, were there to see if this Jesse Owens they had read so much about was equal to the caliber of Eddie Tolan, the former

Michigan sprinter and Olympic champion of 1932, who was attending that meet as a fan. After this day's meet, however, crowds would attend all of Jesse's athletic meets to glimpse one of the most famous athletes of his day.

According to a story Larry Snyder liked to tell, Jesse almost didn't get an opportunity to compete on the day that made him famous. A freak accident weeks before the competition nearly ended the athlete's season prematurely.

Always ready for fun and horseplay, Jesse got into an impromptu wrestling match with a friend and accidentally went rolling down a flight of stairs with the other student atop him. His back felt like it was on fire, and shortly thereafter he couldn't even bend over. The pain frightened him.

Even worse, the ache seemed to travel all over Jesse's body, moving so much that he half-jokingly called it "the rambling pain." As the meet in Ann Arbor, Michigan, grew closer, the pain shifted to the hamstring muscles in one thigh, then down into the knee joint. Terrified that Snyder would have him sit down for a couple of weeks, Jesse refused to tell his coach about the injury, although in retrospect his fears proved unwarranted. Whenever he loosened up and ran heats in practice, the pain and stiffness subsided, only to return at night—but in a lower part of his body. "He was afraid I wouldn't let him compete [but] he was wrong about that," Snyder later said in *The Saturday Evening Post.* "I have always believed that an injury that didn't come from running won't be hurt by running."[2]

Finally, just before the race, the pain settled into Jesse's foot. Then it vacated his body permanently as the team made the trip north to the University of Michigan for the meet on Saturday, May 25.

When the Ohio State team reached the track, Coach Snyder noted with satisfaction that the weather was "perfect" for a meet. The cold temperatures of spring had disappeared overnight, warmed by a hot sun that loosened the muscles of the competitors instead of tightening them. There was only the slightest of winds blowing into Jesse's back as he walked on the track to familiarize himself with its surface. It was little more than a kind breeze, enough to give a slight edge to a sprinter of Jesse's caliber, although still within the three-miles-per-hour (about two-km-per-hour) wind allowance that would negate any records set that day.

The first event was the 100-yard dash. When the starting gun went off, Jesse broke like the thoroughbred horses Coach Riley had taken him to see. All Larry Snyder's tips paid off as Jesse started fast and finished faster. His time was 9.4, tying the world's record established by Frank Wykoff in 1930. He beat a second-place runner from the University of Illinois by 15 feet. As one writer liked to say about him, he ran so smoothly that a cup of water could have been balanced atop his head while he ran.[3]

In retrospect, Jesse's 9.4 time was probably wrong; he likely had run a tenth of a second faster. The race occurred long before the advent of sophisticated timers to clock performances. Three officials timed the race, as was the custom. Two clocked him at 9.3, and one at 9.4. Since the rules stated that only the highest time counted for a record, the 9.4 time was the one that counted. And, instead of stopping the watches when Jesse's chest went over the line—as would happen today—the officials waited until the *back* of his foot crossed it. In short, Jesse Owens's biographer William J. Baker says that the officials were perhaps unduly demanding that day, thereby depriving Jesse of a world record.[4]

If Jesse was disappointed, he didn't show it. He walked over to Larry Snyder and exchanged grins. "I guess I need a backache more often, Coach," said Jesse.[5]

Just ten minutes after Jesse accepted congratulations from his teammates for tying a world record, he limbered up to attempt his second event, the long jump. So that Jesse wouldn't reinjure his back upon impact or be too fatigued for the day's remaining events, his coach told him to make but a single jump.

To have a goal to shoot for, Jesse measured 26 feet 2 inches—the existing world record—and draped a towel over an imaginary line to mark it. He composed himself at the start, launched his body into a perfect spring, and cleared the towel. He had jumped 26 feet 8¼ inches. The crowd gasped as the world record held by Japan's Chuhei Namby fell. Jesse had broken the old mark by better than 6 inches. The jump meant that Jesse was a shoo-in to represent the United States in the 1936 Olympics. The winners of the 1928 and 1932 Olympics—both Americans—had jumped only slightly farther than 25 feet.

"I wish to introduce a world's champion," said long-time Michigan track announcer, Ted Canty, holding up Jesse's hand as if he were a boxing champion. The entire crowd, black and white, pro-Ohio State and pro-Michigan, came to its feet and roared their appreciation for what Jesse had just done.[6]

The athletic director at Michigan State, Ralph Young, had seen many athletes attempt the long jump. Even Young, who was standing alongside the pit at the time, was amazed by such a gargantuan leap. The athlete had jumped so high that he was level with the head of the 5-foot 8-inch Young at the apex of his jump. Snyder wasn't too surprised when the athletic director told him how high Jesse had sprung. "You have to get up

At an NCAA meet in Chicago, Jesse won the long jump and set records in the 100-meter dash, the 200-meter run, and the 220-yard low hurdles.

that high if you are going to jump six inches better than the world's record," Coach Snyder later said.[7]

After completing the jump, Jesse had but twenty minutes to recoup his energy for the 220-yard event. Jesse's heroics in the first two events had won over the partisan crowd, and they gave him respectful silence. No one even shouted out his name. Jesse led the field by 8 yards at the half and 10 yards at the finish, showing his heels to a second-place runner from the University of Iowa.

"Twenty and three-tenth seconds," an official said after conferring with the timers. The silent stadium exploded with cheers as yet another world record for Jesse became official. His time shattered by three-tenths of a second a record set by the University of Nebraska's Roland A. Locke that had stood for eleven years.[8]

The next event was the 2-mile run, followed by the low hurdles. Jesse cornered his coach. "I know this might sound crazy, but I'd like to run the low hurdles, too," he said.

Snyder eyed him, debating whether any athlete could get ready for the demands of the low hurdles after competing in three other events as Jesse had done.

Jesse pleaded with him. "I'll never have another day like this in my life," he said.

"You're right, Jess," said the coach, smiling. But he cautioned Jesse not to try for world-record time. He didn't want the athlete to tighten up by putting too much pressure on himself. "I'll be happy if you can just win the event."[9]

Again Jesse walked to the starting line. Again he beat the finest competition in the Midwest. Again, he had a world record, completing the 220-yard hurdles in 22.6 seconds. The previous mark of 23 seconds flat had been jointly held by Norman Paul and C. R. Brookins.[10]

In spite of Jesse's heroics, he and his Buckeye teammates felt a letdown on the long ride back to Columbus. Michigan had won the meet with 48 points, while Ohio State, with 43½ points, had to be content with second place.[11]

The team caravan headed for Ohio, and Jesse became the most renowned athlete in the country as reporters filed their stories. Reporter Wilfrid Smith of the *Chicago Tribune* called it "one of the greatest exhibitions in the history of track-and-field competition." Never in the space of two brief hours had an athlete ever given such an exhibition, wrote Smith, noting that "his margin of superiority, not only over his immediate contemporaries, but in comparison with the records of all athletes since the days of the Greek Olympics, was . . . astounding." Jesse, at twenty-one, had reached his prime. He had tied one world record and shattered three more.

Unknown to the press, the day of Jesse's magnificent performance, Charles Riley had driven to the meet from Cleveland to see him once again. As those 10,000 fans in Michigan's Ferry Field stood and cheered Jesse as one, in their midst a proud, happy old man cried without shame.[12]

Jesse's athletic career had been on the line, and he had been asked to display not only ability but courage, concentration, and endurance. The young boy who had been intimidated at the 1932 Olympics trials was gone. In his place was a confident, composed adult. In the space of two hours, he had established himself as an athlete who won under pressure. He was the best sprinter and long jumper his country could send to the 1936 Olympic Games in Berlin.

Jesse's 1935 season was impressive also for his consistency week in and week out. He never had a bad outing. In twenty-eight long jump and running events, he won twenty-eight times.

CHAPTER 6

Countdown to the Olympics

Ruth at first was proud of the man who had fathered her daughter, secure with his assurances that they would marry when his financial circumstances allowed. But the adulation of Jesse's newfound fans—many of them attractive young women—upset her. She was hurt and angry when a picture of Jesse in the company of another woman appeared in a Cleveland newspaper. Jesse's "love affairs have become front-page news in the daily newspapers," read an editorial comment in the *Call and Post.*

Clearly, for a time Jesse let fame go to his head, and he took Ruth's love for granted. He failed to take her feelings into account when he began squiring beautiful coeds around Columbus. Justifiably enraged by Jesse's unfaithfulness, she phoned him at the important AAU championships in Nebraska to tell him precisely what she thought about his behavior. To make matters worse, someone had tipped the press off that Jesse had an illegitimate child. A reporter from Cleveland covered the Nebraska meet and told Jesse that he intended to put Gloria's picture on his paper's front page unless he married Ruth.[1]

His concentration destroyed, Jesse competed miserably. He embarrassed his school and himself in both the long jump and 100-meter sprint. Conversely, archrivals Eulace Peacock and Ralph Metcalfe performed spectacularly, putting Jesse's Olympic chances in jeopardy.

On the way home from Nebraska, Jesse resolved to

Jesse and his wife, Ruth, enjoying an evening at the Cotton Club in New York City.

straighten out his life. He finally had come to realize that everything he did was deemed newsworthy. He and Ruth procured a marriage license, and a minister married them that very weekend on July 5, 1935. There would be no honeymoon for the lovers. Jesse left the morning after his wedding night to compete in successive meets in Buffalo; Crystal Beach, Canada; and New York City.

"Minnie Ruth Solomon won the Cupid's Sweepstakes, walking off with the prize . . . Jesse Owens," a Cleveland newspaper pronounced. However, unknown to Ruth, her husband during their long union would demonstrate himself to be both a prize and a prize pain in her heart.[2]

However, the turmoil in Jesse's life was not ended by the wedding ceremony. The anxiety he was experiencing made him tense and tightened his muscles. He performed no better at the post-wedding meets in New York state and Canada than he had done in Nebraska, losing three more races to Eulace Peacock. Jesse's legs might be in perfect shape, but not his head and heart. "Swing wide the gates for a new sports hero," one newspaper said of Peacock.

Jesse's critics began to believe that his failure in the 1932 Olympic Trials seemed destined to recur in 1936. Even Jesse's boyhood hero, Charles Paddock, said publicly that Peacock seemed the better man, attributing Jesse's rapid decline to burnout. The Cleveland black newspapers retracted their former unwavering support of the local hero. They said that perhaps Jesse and Peacock might both go on to star in the Berlin Games.[3]

In 1935, however, Jesse's teammates accorded him a high honor. The Buckeye Bullet was elected captain of the track team, the first African-American in the Big Ten to be so honored. The frail boy had become a strong young man, standing 5 feet 10 inches and weighing a sturdy 165 pounds.

But what should have been a time of happiness instead was a period of crisis. Jesse learned that his amateur status was being questioned by the AAU. If the track governing body declared him a professional athlete, not only his college career but also his Olympic quest would be over.

Jesse's newest problem, ironically, came about because he had become so beloved. Supporters of Ohio State track-and-field wanted to keep him happy. Shortly after the Christmas holidays the previous year, Jesse had quit his elevator operator job for a prestigious page boy job in the Ohio State Senate. There was nothing secretive about it. Jesse proudly posed for photographs, dressed in a suit with a fashionable silk hankerchief in a breast pocket. He had—by virtue of his athletic accomplishments—acquired a political position traditionally taken by young white athletes from Ohio State. He got the page boy job through the influence of a sister who worked for a Cleveland politician as a ward captain. On the surface, he had achieved yet another victory for African-Americans.

The controversy began when his sister arranged for her brother to draw a weekly $21 paycheck during the summer as an honorary page while he was on the road competing. Under such a guise, Ohio taxpayers paid his way to track meets in California in 1935. AAU investigators learned of the situation and were ready to declare Jesse a professional athlete if they determined that he had been given a so-called "sweetheart deal"— getting paid for work he didn't do simply because he was an athlete. Without question, under the NCAA rules of the 1990s, both Jesse and Ohio State would have been in deep trouble.[4]

For a short period of time, Jesse (left) worked as a senate page in Ohio. This job would call his amateur status into question.

But big-time college athletics was still in its infancy, and officials tended to handle all infractions on a case-by-case basis. In his favor, Jesse had many supporters who liked him as an athlete and a person and were willing to go to bat for him. Jesse testified in Cleveland on August 12 before the AAU. The local members of that organization assured the investigating team that the athlete was a person of fine character.

The meeting must have terrified this son of former sharecroppers who thought his Olympic dreams might evaporate. He had to testify before an all-white jury committee with his entire future on the line. That committee recommended to the national body that Jesse's amateur status be preserved on condition that he reimburse the state $159, which he readily agreed to do. But the local committee was not the final arbiter, and the national executive branch of the AAU then took over the investigation.

While the AAU inquiry dragged on during the fall quarter of 1935, Jesse returned to Ohio State for his third year. Academically, he had not earned sufficient credits to be declared a junior.

At that time, the track world was abuzz with rumors that the United States might refuse to participate in the German Olympics to protest the ill treatment of Jewish citizens under German Chancellor Adolf Hitler's regime. The AAU, in particular, supported a boycott, particularly after Hitler no longer recognized Jews as citizens and had deprived them of virtually all civil rights. The International Olympic Committee (IOC) and the American Olympic Committee were opposed to a boycott. Members argued that politics had no place in sport.

Across the ocean, the ruling Nazis in Germany had angry discussions about participating in the Games. They objected to mingling with Negroes, saying that blacks belonged to an inferior "primitive" race. The vehemence of many Nazis toward blacks rivaled that of the American Ku Klux Klan. Germany's relatively small black population suffered large-scale discrimination during the mid-thirties, according to historian Robert Waite.

"Negroes have no place at an Olympiad," declared one German writer, saying that it was unfortunate that athletes from the so-called superior race had to compete "against unfree blacks . . . for the victory wreath."

The writer expressed anger that the Americans were bringing blacks such as Jesse Owens and Ralph Metcalfe to the 1936 Games. "This is an unparalleled disgrace and degradation," wrote the German commentator. "The ancient Greeks would turn in their graves if they knew what modern men have made out of their holy . . . Games." He concluded that the IOC had a responsibility to protect German athletes from the taint of associating with Negro athletes.

"The blacks must be excluded," he said. "We expect nothing less."[5]

Reluctantly, Hitler finally caved in to the IOC on the matter of blacks competing in the Games. He gave his personal pledge that Germany would welcome people of all races and religions. Otherwise, his nation would have lost the right to sponsor the Olympics. Perhaps to downplay the success that these U.S. members of the supposed "primitive" race were expected to have, German scientists tried to dehumanize Jesse Owens. Carrying their theories on race to extremes, they put forth an inane theory that his ability in running sports came from bone conformation and an animal-like muscular energy.

In short, these Nazi scientists were unwilling to give Jesse his due. They were unable to admit that while it was true that he was blessed with genes that gave him unmatched physical attributes, his success was also attributable to hard training, the ability to benefit from coaching, and his own determination. Later in life, Jesse himself debunked the notion that blacks had some sporting advantage built into their genes. "There is no difference between the races," he insisted. "If the black athlete has been better than his white counterpart, it's because he's hungrier—he wants it more." [6]

Hitler himself subscribed to such racist theories. He erroneously believed that blacks lacked the intellectual capacities to go with their physical gifts.

But while Jesse may have had difficulties in school, no one who knew him doubted his intelligence. While at Ohio State, he was always in demand as a speaker. Radio interviewers found him warm and engaging, and his views on a possible U.S. boycott of the 1936 Olympic Games were often solicited by print journalists. One of the nation's largest newspapers, the *Chicago Defender*, gave its readers regular coverage of Jesse's views and talks at various schools and colleges.[7]

Jesse at first publicly recommended a U.S. boycott of the Games, apparently willing to forego his dream of collecting Olympic gold medals in order to protest racism and anti-Semitism. His trusted coach and friend, Larry Snyder, changed Jesse's mind, reminding him that black athletes were occasionally not allowed to participate in prestigious U.S. meets. Why boycott a German sports contest when conditions are no better in your own country? Snyder argued. He urged Jesse not to end up a martyr for a political cause. The passion of Snyder's convictions stopped Jesse's talk of boycotting Germany, but from then on he became much more serious about addressing racial inequities in his native country.[8]

After many months the AAU ended its investigation into Jesse's amateur status. The investigation concluded that improprieties had been made by those who offered Jesse a page job without requiring him to work, but that he himself had not intentionally broken any rules. The upshot was that he retained his eligibility, although the long, drawn-out process sapped his energies and made concentrating difficult in the classroom. He went on academic probation and was prevented from participating in track over the winter quarter. In addition, his character had been questioned—the first of several times it would come under scrutiny during his lifetime. The only good news was that Jesse had little trouble making a prestigious All-America team.[9]

The controversy had one positive aspect. Jesse seems to have matured as a person as a result of enduring these controversies. He began to be aware of the importance of protecting his public image by behaving always as a role model for the young people who idolized him. He began to behave with dignity, even applying himself better to his studies. His grades, while not high, were sufficient to reinstate his eligibility for the spring outdoor track season.

Jesse's first public display of grace and maturity occurred during a race in Cleveland against Eulace Peacock. This particular indoor meet was billed as a battle between America's two fastest men. Jesse was out to atone for his losses to Peacock the previous summer.

Significantly, the sprint races required runners to use primitive starting blocks that were far below the standards of those used today. He and Peacock lined up, the starter's gun boomed, and Jesse roared down the track to win an easy victory.

Jesse only savored the win for a moment, learning that Peacock's starting blocks had failed him, causing him to stumble at the start and drop out of the event. Rather than take a tainted victory, Jesse quietly insisted that the race be run over.

Six thousand fans cheered this unprecedented display of good sportsmanship. The runners again took their positions. The starter's gun sounded, and both men hit the tape seemingly at the same time, although the judges ruled that Peacock had won by the briefest of margins. Nonetheless, although he lost the match, Jesse had shown a spirit of decency and fair play that he would demonstrate time and again during his career. The *Cleveland Call and Post* duly reported Jesse's conduct to its readers. Although he wanted nothing in this world so much as to compete in the Olympics, he was going to get there on his own merits, not through an opponent's misfortune, Jesse's actions clearly said.

Unfortunately for Peacock, that race was his swan song. A burly man with an overabundant appetite, he failed to train properly for the Olympics. He ballooned to nearly 190 pounds while he was inactive with a minor leg injury before the trials in 1936.

The long-awaited, head-to-head battle between the two champions, Jesse and Peacock, failed to materialize. The muscular Peacock, in less than his best shape, tore a hamstring at the Penn Relays in Philadelphia. This time, not even the gentlemanly Jesse could give his rival a second chance. Had the fates been kinder, Peacock might have become America's great hope in the Olympic running events, leaving only the long jump for Jesse to win. Jesse's ability to keep himself in superior physical condition at all times kept him from ever sustaining more than minor injuries.

At the Penn Relays, Jesse once again seemed mentally ready to pursue his long-held Olympic dreams. He went back to Ohio State with first-place finishes in the 100-meter sprint and long jump, as well as running anchor on a Buckeye win in the 400-meter relays—the same event that had crippled Eulace Peacock.

Once again the front-runner, Jesse began to notice

a new tone to the questions reporters asked him. More and more questions addressed the issue of race. It became apparent that many of America's best amateur athletes in 1936 were African-Americans and nineteen blacks made the Olympic squad bound for Berlin. In addition to Jesse and Metcalfe, runners Archie Williams, Jimmy LuValle, and Mack Robinson were highly talented black men. Dave Albritton, Jesse's friend, was a promising high jumper. And Jesse's main competition in the long jump, Johnny Brooks, was black.[10]

Many sportswriters created an "us versus them" atmosphere, putting all blacks into a single category and giving them labels such as "our Ethiopian troops" under the guise of snappy journalistic writing. "We may have to comb Africa again for sure winners," said one respected journalist—as if hundreds of years of slavery could be reduced to some sort of athletic talent search.[11]

Also implicit in such words was the conscious or unconscious desire to warn American whites that they were in pretty sad shape if it took American blacks to uphold the athletic honor of the United States. A sensitive man, Jesse was aware of the distinctions the press was making about him, but he kept following Larry Snyder's advice not to make waves.

Seen in retrospect, America's two greatest heroes in international competition during the 1930s happened to be black men. One was the boxer Joe Louis, who had become the world heavyweight champion at twenty-three years old. The other was Jesse. As if trying to downplay Louis's importance, the press treated him too often as a caricature, exaggerating his drawling dialect to make him sound as ignorant as a stereotypical "darkie." A racist journalist for the *Atlanta Journal* nicknamed him "the Pet Pickaninny.[12]

Jesse, on the other hand, was a natural speaker whose perfect voice, enunciation, and raw intelligence made it impossible to turn him into a caricature. The simple fact is that many Americans of all races identified with the success of these black athletes. Some newspaper men downplayed their importance by labeling them "a credit to their race." More accurately, they were a credit to the entire nation, keeping American morale high during the uncertain times between the Great Depression and World War II. Because both Jesse and Louis had overcome poor childhoods in Alabama, they were role models for all Americans who believed in the American Dream.

In the summer of 1936, many people in the United States put their hopes on Jesse after Peacock's injury eliminated him from competition. The Olympics were taking place soon after America had suffered a galling defeat in international competition. On July 18, a sluggish Joe Louis—overconfident, in less-than-top condition, and undertrained—had suffered an embarrassing defeat in Yankee Stadium to a well-trained underdog challenger from Germany, Max Schmeling. The Nazi government used the fight to point out supposed superiority of Germany over the United States.

"How much this has accomplished for the German cause should not be understated," reported a writer for a leading German publication. A movie of the Louis-Schmeling fight "played to full houses all over Germany," according to Louis's biographer, Chris Mead. Schmeling himself came to enjoy his role as "the archapostle of the doctrine of Aryan superiority over an inferior race," reported Arthur Daley of *The New York Times*. The boxer even kept a framed and autographed portrait of Hitler in his living room.[13]

German morale was high as final preparations for the Olympics were made. Hitler's armies had recently occupied the Rhineland of France. He was about to sign an alliance with Fascist dictator Benito Mussolini of Italy, who himself recently had invaded Ethiopia and brutalized its black citizens. In contrast, many Americans looked to Jesse Owens, already billed by some as "the world's fastest human," to redeem American honor. The pressure on the 22-year-old college student was immense as he headed from Columbus to the Olympic Trials in New York City, hoping to fare far better than he had in 1932. In a sense, Jesse was redeeming not only his own pride but his country's.

One day during the summer of 1936, Jesse experienced a revelation that told him both how far he had come and how much he had changed. He glanced at a local newspaper while eating breakfast with his wife and daughter and saw a photograph of himself staring back at him.

"What shocked me wasn't that my picture was on the front page," he later admitted. "It was that I'd gotten *used* to seeing it there."[14]

A second revelation was more dramatic. America's best sprinter attended a banquet with America's best home-run hitter, Babe Ruth, whose great career was nearing its end. As Jesse later recalled the incident, he felt an instant bond with the white baseball player, perhaps because Ruth too had been reared in poverty and used sports to make a name for himself.

"You gonna win at the Olympics, Jesse?" Ruth asked him while both were seated at the head table.

Jesse answered modestly, trying not to seem "uppity" to this white superstar. "Gonna try."

Ruth answered with an expletive. "Everybody *tries*," he croaked. "I *succeed*. Want to know why?"

Jesse nodded.

"I hit sixty home runs . . . because I *know* I'm going to hit a home run just about every time I swing that

64

bat," said Ruth. "I'm surprised when I *don't*. . . . Because *I* know it, the pitchers know it too. They're pretty sure I'm going to hit a homer every time."

Ruth laughed, as did Jesse, who filed away the story to use in his memoirs. Ever after, Jesse was a great believer in inner confidence, knowing beforehand that he would win a race or long jump. Opponents saw the confidence in him, and like Ruth's pitchers, were sometimes beaten before they knelt at the starting line.[15]

CHAPTER 7

Eve of the Olympic Games

The big sports story at the Olympic Trials held in New York at Randall's Island sports complex was Eulace Peacock's valiant attempt to compete against Jesse in the long jump and sprints. Peacock's injured leg was swathed in tape, and his performances were painful for Jesse and other competitors to watch. In spite of his injuries, the athlete's show of heart inspired everyone who watched him. Nonetheless, Peacock failed miserably in every jump and race he attempted.

Jesse, on the other hand, had been carefully brought along by Coach Larry Snyder. He was strong, alert, and experienced, making it clear to the track world that Jesse Owens was on one level, while other athletes were on a lower level. He won the long jump and both the 100-meter and 200-meter sprints.

Jesse was one of an unprecedented nineteen blacks to make the cut for the final U.S. Olympic team. Since only five blacks had made the team in 1932, members of the black press were exuberant, one even proclaiming that the selections atoned for Joe Louis's loss to Max Schmeling. Millions of young black children had an authentic sports hero to worship in Jesse. The *Baltimore Afro-American* ran a picture of Jesse on its front page on June 27. The extraordinary size of the photograph clearly indicated that here was a larger-than-life figure.

Years later, Jesse himself would say that "until the thirties, the Negro had no image to point to." He said

66

Eulace Peacock was often stiff competition for Jesse. Here he is shown getting off to a quick start in the 100-meter dash.

that he and Louis rode "the wave of newfound pride that the Negro had then."[1]

A magazine for educated African-Americans called *The Crisis* carried an editorial on the benefits all blacks derived from the success of Joe Louis and Jesse Owens. The publication said that while it wished to avoid the error of proclaiming that the victory of these two blacks somehow guaranteed the future success of all blacks, nonetheless the two "have aided materially in altering the usual appraisal of Negroes by the rank and file of the American public." Simply by drawing attention to their race, they have done a great service, said the writer.

"Those who maintain that a Negro historian or editor or philosopher or scientist or composer or singer or poet or painter is more important than a great athlete are on sound ground, but they would be foolish to maintain that these worthy individuals have more power for influence than the athletes," concluded the editorial. "After all, it is not the infinitesimal intellectual America which needs conversion on the race problem; it is the rank and file, the ones who never read a book by Du Bois, or heard a lecture by [NAACP leader] James Weldon Johnson, or scanned a poem of Countee Cullen, or heard a song by [opera contralto] Marian Anderson, or waded through a scholarly treatise. . . . For these millions, who hold the solution of the race problem in their hands, the beautiful breasting of a tape by Jesse Owens and the thud of a glove on the hand of Joe Louis carry more 'interracial education' than all the erudite philosophy ever written on race."[2]

His mind on athletics, Jesse said little if anything about his feelings on race at that time. Those statements would come later as he grew and matured.

At the time, he was overjoyed that his lifelong dream of reaching the Olympics was turning into reality. To add to his satisfaction, his boyhood friend David Albritton had made the team in the high jump—just as they had dreamed back in high school. So did Jesse's longtime friendly rival in sprint events, Ralph Metcalfe.

Some of the satisfaction that black Americans felt in the selection of so many blacks to the Olympic squad was tempered by Hilter's racist ravings. Hitler predicted that such "inferior" Americans would be easy prey for what he assumed were superior German athletes. The Germans boasted that their long jumper, Luz Long, was a "super-athlete" who would vanquish Jesse in that important event.[3]

"We were everything Hitler hated," Jesse said in his autobiography. "In particular, Hitler hated my skin."[4]

The voyage on the liner SS *Manhattan* was the first time Jesse had ever left American soil. He packed the

Jesse (center) shown along with the other members of the 1936 Olympic track team.

only suit he owned, a natty, gangster-style pinstripe suit, and so many stylish pants and shirts that his Olympic shipmates voted him "best dressed" in a poll they conducted. Nonetheless, he had no money to spend on frills aboard ship. He sailed with but $8 in his pocket.[5]

After departure on July 15, 1936, Jesse's heart ached to pick up the phone and talk to his wife and parents, but this was, of course, impossible. He was lonely, but also afraid. He wanted to share his feelings about the fear that threatened to paralyze him with his teammates, but he could not. He had received too much publicity and was considered a team leader. What would it do to team morale if he showed fear? He kept his loneliness and fears to himself. His friend, Ralph Metcalfe, behaved like the Olympic veteran he was, calming the nerves of Jesse and the other blacks with a stirring speech that urged them not to take the bait of any reporters to comment on Hitler and his Nazis. They were there to win gold medals for their nation.

"That led to our success," Jesse told a Chicago newspaper reporter in 1978 after Metcalfe died. "He calmed our fears. He was the guy who did it for us."[6]

As the most famous male athlete on board, Jesse knew that the fans, reporters, and even German Chancellor Adolf Hitler were hearing reports from the press about him. He conducted himself well on the trip, keeping a low-key presence, but was ill with frequent seasickness and a nasty cold that kept him bedridden part of the trip. Because Jesse already had four world records in track, the perfectionist in him felt that he had to surpass his previous accomplishments. He used the ship's deck to stretch to keep his muscles loose. Nonetheless, even though he was confined to his quarters much of the trip, he kept his sense of humor and was voted the second most popular athlete on the liner, behind marathoner Glenn Cunningham.[7]

Six thousand athletes from fifty-three nations reached Berlin that August. Every athlete knew that the Nazis had proclaimed themselves the saviors of a Germany that had been humbled by its defeat during World War I. But Jesse and his teammates had no idea that America and Germany were on the brink of competing with bullets instead of games. Historian Robert Waite says it isn't surprising that the American Olympians lacked insight into the true nature of Adolf Hitler.

"How would the Olympians recognize it?" said Waite. "The British and other European governments didn't recognize it. These governments were still trying to deal with Hitler as a responsible statesman. The arrests of Jews, for example, were not as widespread as they would become later on."[8]

No other nation knew precisely what these Olympic Games meant to Adolf Hitler and the Nazi Party. Hitler expected German athletes to run roughshod over the competition, and the party had spent large sums to train and house the finest white, Christian athletes. Only two Jewish athletes wore the German Olympic uniform. Three years earlier, Hitler had mandated that no Jew could use private or public sports facilities, thereby making it difficult for Jewish athletes to train and make the team.[9]

"The Olympics were going to be proof of the justification of Hitler's racial system," says Waite. "It was the foundation for his whole political system. The fundamental principal underlying Hitler's idea of Nazi Germany was the idea of the racial community."

In other words, Hitler had a very narrow concept of the sort of people who would be in control of Germany and the world one day, says Waite. Hitler pictured an ideal northern European man and woman who were light-skinned, Anglo-Saxon, fair-haired and blue-eyed. He called such people Aryans. Jews and to a lesser extent blacks, in the opinion of the Nazis, had to be eliminated because they would detract from the overall strength and power of Germany. Hitler didn't want his country to become a so-called "melting pot" of various peoples, as the United States had become.

Thus, for Hitler and his party, the "Nazi Olympics" symbolized far more than a mere athletic competition. It was imperative that German athletes outclass all competitors. Coupled with the German Schmeling's defeat of Louis, these Games were of major political and cultural significance," said Games historian Richard D. Mandell.[10]

Only a few perceptive non-German visitors to the Games had an inkling that these Olympics foreshadowed the horrors of World War II. "There seemed to be something ominous in [the pageantry]," wrote visiting American novelist Thomas Wolfe. "One sensed a stupendous concentration of effort, a tremendous drawing together and ordering in the vast collective power of the whole land. And the thing that made it seem ominous was that it so evidently went beyond what the Games themselves demanded. The Games were overshadowed, and were no longer merely sporting competitions to which other nations had sent their chosen teams. They became, day after day, an orderly and overwhelming demonstration in which the whole of Germany had been schooled and disciplined. It was as if the Games had been chosen as a symbol of the new collective might, a means of showing to the world in concrete terms what this new [Nazi] power had come to be."[11]

Journalist Grantland Rice, old enough to remember the events of World War I with clarity, felt intimidated by what he believed were unmistakable preparations for war in Berlin. He saw that Nazi banners with the easily recognized black swastika insignia competed with Olympic flags for space. Even a walk around the block could not be made without the chilling sight of armed soldiers.

Jesse, confined to the Olympic Village, knew little of the political climate. Instead, he was impressed with German hospitality when he first reached the Olympic village at Döberitz, a town thirty minutes by car from the stadium, which had been built in the beautiful wooded countryside. The athletes were greeted by members of Hitler Youth, a paramilitary organization composed of young people dedicated to Nazi ideals, who had been instructed to show the visiting athletes both respect and courtesy.

The Germans made sure that Jesse and his fellow Americans found their rooms comfortable and the dormitory food excellent. At night, athletes could see their own victories and losses in newsreels. A television in the village—the first that Jesse had seen—broadcast the Games, although with less than perfect reception. Music by the Berlin Philharmonic Orchestra, a fireworks display, cabaret acts, movies, and variety acts were provided for nightly entertainment. Curiously, the responsibility for organizing the Olympic Village was put at least for a time in the hands of Wolfgang Fürstner, who was Jewish.[12]

The Games were the most popular attraction in Germany. Although 3.4 million tickets had been sold, many more fans could not get tickets. To reach everyone, the Nazis placed loudspeakers throughout the city from which blared the voice of a German announcer calling the events. The city fathers of Berlin developed sophisticated plans to handle the massive crowds and their automobiles. There never were traffic jams such as those that had clogged Los Angeles during the 1932 Olympics. The only thing the Germans had overlooked was the need for a rest area for competitors at the stadium. Athletes such as Jesse who competed in multiple events did not have the time to get all the way back to the village for midday meals. Instead of nourishing hot lunches, he had to make do with eating the rather unappealing sandwiches and warm milk that he and Larry Snyder brought with them from the village.[13]

In the months before the Olympics, fearful that the International Olympic Committee might assign the Games to another country if its policies against Jews became too blatant, the Nazis did everything possible to deflect world criticism away from the German political party's abject record on human rights issues. Just as

In Germany, many Jewish businesses were boycotted during Adolf Hitler's reign.

blacks back home in America had to endure signs in many public places that said they were unwelcome, so too in the early 1930s had Jews found similar signs hanging in German business establishments. But just prior to the Games the signs came down, and the government temporarily lifted its ban on books by Jewish authors.

Hitler, as it turned out, was only waiting for the Games to end before he resumed and accelerated his persecution of Jews. The dictator believed that God had ordained him to annihilate the Jews for the "crime" of worshiping as their ancestors before them had done."[14]

In addition, the goodwill engendered by the Olympics allowed Hitler to continue buying and selling strategic materials needed for arms production. "Hitler was gearing up for war and realized that foreign trade was still very important," notes Robert Waite. "Hitler didn't want to alienate completely the international community."

The Games were a perfect propaganda tool for the Germans. Hitler took advantage of every opportunity to showcase supposed superiority in technology and architecture. He ordered a stadium built in Berlin for the Olympics that was superior to the Los Angeles Coliseum used for the 1932 Games. It had a seating capacity of 110,000, as well as an Olympic indoor swimmng pool with seating for 20,000. The great German composer Richard Strauss penned an Olympic theme song to inspire the athletes and the crowd during the Opening Day ceremonies.

There was much public pressure for the United States to boycott the Games, as the nation would do in 1980 to protest the former Soviet Union's aggression in Afghanistan. Many speeches were made insisting that America needed to protest the Nazi oppression of Jews. However, the IOC contended successfully that politics had no part in the world's most prestigious sporting event. When, in a then-unrivaled display of splendor, the Nazis reinstituted the ancient custom of lighting a torch in Olympia, Greece, and then transported it by relay teams across seven nations to the Berlin stadium, U.S. Olympic Committee President Avery Brundage was effusive in his praise of the host. "No nation since ancient Greece has captured the true Olympic spirit as has Germany," he said.

One of Brundage's biggest critics, Larry Snyder, attended the Olympic Games in an unofficial capacity. He accompanied Jesse to Berlin to oversee his workouts but paid his own expenses. His pep talks sometimes tended to be sentimental. At Ohio State, both coach and athlete wept after one inspirational session, he told *The Saturday Evening Post*.[15]

Snyder feared the sensitive Jesse might feel shaken when he stepped into the stadium; the coach expected the American star to be frostily treated by the pro-German crowd. But to Snyder's amazement, fans in Berlin greeted Jesse with affection and enthusiasm.

Unknown to the coach, stories with photographs of Jesse had appeared many times in prominent German publications. The athlete was an international celebrity. The Germans chanted his name over and over, pronouncing it "Yesseh Ohvens," politely stopping when it was his turn to compete so that they wouldn't throw off his rhythm.

"Enthusiasm about the Negro contingency centers mainly around Owens," noted one U.S. reporter. "None of the others enjoy anything approaching his popularity." [16]

Nonetheless, Jesse was grateful that Snyder had accompanied him. One of the official U.S. Olympic track coaches, the University of Pennsylvania's Lawson Robertson, asked Jesse to alter his running style. Like other coaches in the international community, Robertson was perplexed by Jesse's unusual stride; he never ran with knees high as other world-class sprinters did.[17] Robertson's request was ill-timed and ill-advised, disturbing Jesse's concentration.

Jesse was too well-mannered to confront Robertson, but he told Snyder who protested such interference. Robertson backed down, and Jesse worked out without further "help" from him.

In addition, Snyder tried to shield Jesse from fans and foreign athletes who mobbed him at the village and stadium. Snyder was powerless to stop the invasion of Jesse's privacy at the village, but officials prohibited autograph-seeking during workouts at the stadium.

Nonetheless, Jesse's temperament was so naturally amiable that he honored requests—as if it were the autograph seekers who were doing something nice by asking him. He befriended one small German girl, thirteen-year-old Ina Beyer, who took part in the colorful Olympic ceremonies. The two became pals, and Jesse challenged her to teach him German. Ina had long braids and Jesse repeatedly asked her, "What are these?" Again and again she would tell him the German term, *Tsöpfe*. But to her merriment and his frustration, he could never get the term right.[18]

Jesse's popularity was entirely without precedent. He awoke in the morning to find people shoving autograph books through his open bedroom window. Larry Snyder took it upon himself to remind Jesse to keep things in perspective, feeling that if the athlete started believing his press clippings, he'd lose his competitive edge. "He was too likable . . . to let himself be spoiled," Snyder explained. "And I wasn't going to allow it if I could help it."[19]

Even the victorious German boxer Max Schmeling came to the village to gawk at Jesse and engage him in conversation. Jesse's loyalties decidely were with Joe Louis. "Inwardly many of us were trying to atone for Joe's loss," Jesse later said. Schmeling's presence inspired the black athletes to do their best; it failed to intimidate them. Ironically, the boxer thought that the mobbing of Jesse by German fans was evidence enough that the German people had no racist tendencies. He said that Jesse's popularity was evidence that "Germans are the fairest people in the world."[20]

Jesse admitted that his first sight of Luz Long, the great German long jumper, awed him. Long was putting on a spectacular show of his talents during a workout as Jesse and the American squad arrived to practice for the first time in the unfamiliar German stadium.

"He indeed was a supreme example of Aryan perfection," Jesse later recalled. "Taller than I was . . . the blue-eyed, sandy-haired Long was one of those rare athletic happenings you come to recognize after years in competition—a perfectly proportioned body, every lithe but powerful cord a celebration of pulsing natural muscle, stunningly compressed and honed by tens of thousands of obvious hours of sweat and determination."[21]

Never before had Jesse seen a competitor who more closely resembled those racehorses that Coach Riley had asked him to study. When he watched his rival take a practice jump, Long seemed to float in the air forever before landing feet-first in the farthest end of the gravel pit.

A long jumper from another nation recognized Jesse and commiserated with him. "If they were measuring what that German did, it might be a new [world] record," he said. Jesse agreed with that assessment.[22]

Nonetheless, in person Long turned out to be a modest and unassuming athlete. He and Jesse liked one another at first handshake. Other German athletes were equally quick to introduce themselves. One of Jesse's main rivals in the sprint events, Erich Borchmeyer, made a point of approaching Jesse to speak with him in broken English. The brawny, broad-chested Borchmeyer knew what it was like to compete in a strange land and tried to make Jesse feel comfortable. Four years earlier, Borchmeyer had represented Germany in the sprint events at the Los Angeles Olympics.

While they chatted, Borchmeyer's coach walked over to inspect Jesse. He never said a word, only regarded the American runner's legs as closely as if they were pinned under a microscope, recalled Larry Snyder with amusement in an article he wrote about Jesse for *The Saturday Evening Post*. "Jesse's legs are no different from any other athlete's legs," said Snyder, "except that they are better formed than any legs I have ever seen in eight years of running and ten of coaching." To settle the question, a Cleveland doctor examined Jesse in 1935. "He X-rayed Owens's leg bones, measured his arms, trunk, head and legs," later wrote reporter Gay Talese of *The New York Times*. He concluded that the athlete's successes were due to superior training and outstanding courage, not some bodily trait peculiar to his race.[23]

In spite of so much attention, Jesse quickly acclimatized himself in Berlin. The American Olympic team, unlike those of some nations, had arrived several days before the Games, enabling them to get used to life in the stadium and village.

Even a veteran athlete like Jesse found it difficult to adjust to the inclement weather, however. That August of 1936 in Europe was plagued by winds, rain, unseasonable cold temperatures, and high humidity. Jesse and the other athletes, when not competing, kept their sweatsuits on to lessen the chance of tearing or straining a muscle. He and Ralph Metcalfe also kept warm by wrapping wool blankets around themselves. When he was tired, Jesse rested on cots appropriated from a local Red Cross station. When the cool, muggy weather made his muscles tighten, he made use of the one rubdown table in the American resting room, until an enterprising member of the team found an extra table in the unused dressing room that had been assigned to Spain.[24]

Jesse was fully aware of the horrific irony. Civil war had broken out in that country a few weeks earlier. Spanish athletes were fighting for their lives while athletes in Germany were fighting for medals.

CHAPTER 8
Hitler's Olympic Games

At the Opening Ceremonies it was clear that tension existed between the visiting American team and their Nazi hosts. Unlike some of the visiting teams who gave Adolph Hitler a Nazi salute, the squad refused to dip the U.S. flag in salute while passing his stand in review. Many Germans angrily stamped their feet at what they construed to be a deliberate insult.[1]

But German fans held no animosity toward Jesse Owens. The American's quest for Olympic immortality began the afternoon of August 2, 1936. He was ecstatic to learn that he would not have to run until the twelfth and final qualifying heat in his opening event, the 100 meters. He stood on the sidelines and practiced getting a fast start every time the starter's gun sounded. The delay afforded him a wonderful advantage to observe the best runners in the first eleven heats, committing their respective running styles to memory.

Germany's Eric Borchmeyer captivated Jesse. Had Borchmeyer been born an American, he would have been a star running back in football. He was massive and powerful like Eulace Peacock and Ralph Metcalfe. His thigh and calf muscles bulged, and he had the biceps of a bodybuilder. Jesse saw Hitler and his entourage cheer wildly when Borchmeyer won his heat in 10.7 seconds.

Another runner to beat was Frank Wykoff, an athlete from California whose 1930 record of 9.4 in the 100-yard dash had been tied by Jesse in his memorable

The Olympic torch being brought into the stadium in Berlin.

1935 meet at the University of Michigan. Although six years past his running prime, Wykoff was still formidable, easily winning his heat in 10.6. Finally, a Dutch sprinter named Martinus Osendarp captured his heat in 10.5, the best time registered in the sprints thus far. As Jesse removed his warm-up outfit to take his turn, he knew that Osendarp's mark would be the one he'd have to try to beat in his own qualifying round.[1]

Before taking his mark in the twelfth heat, Jesse used a silver trowel—a souvenir from the German sponsors of the Games—to scoop small starting holes for his feet. Jesse kept his face expressionless, but he saw that recent rains had damaged the track, making conditions less than optimum for a record-setting run.

The German starter commanded Jesse and the rest of the field to get ready. The runner's Adam's apple bobbed in his neck, but otherwise he displayed no nerves. Unlike some of the other athletes, Jesse took only a second to settle into a comfortable starting stance.

The gun sounded, and Jesse strode powerfully forward, keeping his body low for the first third of the course. In a couple of heartbeats, the race was over. Jesse learned he had qualified with a time of 10.2 seconds. At first the crowd thought that Jesse had established new world and Olympic records, but officials ruled otherwise. They claimed that the run had been aided by the wind at Jesse's back. The press tried to get Jesse to say that the German officials had robbed him, but he kept his composure. He insisted that the race had been fairly conducted.[2]

Everywhere Jesse walked he ran into movie cameras. In addition to newsreel shooters, he was followed by the film crew of a famous documentary maker, Leni Riefenstahl. She had an eye for the human body like that of a sculptor, focusing her cameras on athletes such as Jesse who were particularly well built. In one closeup before a race, the camera captured the contrast between Jesse's massive, rippling thighs and calves and his small, childlike feet and tiny ankles.

Not only the press, but the children Jesse talked to in the thousands of lectures he would give as an adult, were baffled by those tiny feet. "How could Jesse Owens run so fast with small foots?" a young Abidjanian boy once timidly asked him.

Jesse had laughed, not minding such honest inquisitiveness from a child. "Because I didn't have as much to lift up or to put down," he told the boy.[3]

On that first day of competition, one other great American athlete competed, although her accomplishments were overshadowed by the attention paid to Jesse. Helen Stephens—America's greatest female runner of the era—outdistanced her competition in a 100-meter elimination heat by 30 feet. Had officials not ruled that the run was wind-aided, her 11.4 time would have set world and Olympic marks. Afterward, the world's fastest woman—a gifted runner from Missouri—posed for photographs with Jesse, the fastest man.

Jesse's first run had ended shortly before noon. In the afternoon, Hitler and an entourage that included filmmaker Riefenstahl and boxing hero Schmeling took their seats in the dictator's personal box. The shout from the Germans in the crowd at their first sight of the Nazi leader matched the reception given to Jesse's brilliant run in the first heat.[4]

Hitler and his entourage gathered in his private box in time to view the elimination round in the shotput. He was not disappointed. Germany went on to win a first-place medal in the event. Footage taken by Riefenstahl's crew shows the German dictator celebrating a win with the exuberance of a common fan.

Hitler's enthusiasm made him commit a serious diplomatic blunder. He invited four German medalists to his box to receive them as the crowd screamed its approval. And when an athlete from Finland won a gold medal in the 10,000-meter event, the dictator also graciously received this foreigner in his box.[5]

Before the Olympics, Hitler was confident that his well-trained Aryans would dominate the Games. Consequently, he found himself in the midst of a political predicament when American black athletes showed signs of dominating their respective events. "He was in the limelight and had to be careful," says historian Robert Waite.

Because Hitler had denounced the handful of blacks living in Germany, he feared he would lose face with Nazi Party leaders if he publicly congratulated a black athlete. The dictator's hatred of blacks was genuine. He later would inter some blacks in concentration camps during the 1940s, says Waite.[6]

Nonetheless, having invited one foreigner to his box, Hitler found himself in an uncomfortable situation on the very first afternoon of competition when it looked as though one of two black Americans—Cornelius Johnson or Jesse's friend David Albritton—would win the high jump. If the dictator failed to invite a black winner to his box after congratulating a Finn, the Americans would say their star had been snubbed.

On the field, Albritton had no thoughts of politics. According to the *Chicago Defender*, a black newspaper, he was trying to gain an advantage by upsetting the concentration of Johnson, an athlete who liked to work fast without interruptions. The night before, Jesse had encouraged his friend and roommate Albritton to try delaying tactics such as tying and untying and retying his track shoes. Jesse hoped Johnson might get annoyed and rattled. The trick was not all that unusual. Olympic athletes frequently tried psychological ploys to gain an edge over a rival.

Johnson, however, ignored Albritton. He set an Olympic record with a jump of 6 feet 8 inches, one that wouldn't be erased until 1952 by another American, Walter Davis. Albritton settled for a silver medal.

Before the national anthem could be played, Hitler quickly left the stadium, leaving a representative to lamely try to convince the press that his departure time had been prearranged. Many American newspapers, including *The New York Times* refused to accept the excuse, mentioning the snub of Cornelius Johnson in a headline.

Overnight, the episode threatened to cause an international furor until Hitler promised the IOC that he would publicly congratulate no more athletes—even German medalists. The solution disturbed many reporters, particularly members of the black press in America, who wanted the dictator to recognize the accomplishments of African-American Olympians.

Jesse thought little of the controversy when he awoke the morning of the second day of competition. He put his energies into thoughts of the biggest single race in his life, the finals of the 100-meter dash. "We weren't there to worry about Hitler," he later would say. His competition would have intimidated a lesser man. In addition to Osendarp of Holland and Borchmeyer of Germany, he would need to defeat Ralph Metcalfe and Frank Wykoff on his own American squad. The sixth man rounding out the field was Sweden's Hans Strandberg.[7]

The track was in much worse condition than it had been twenty-four hours earlier. Jesse munched on a soggy steak sandwich and guzzled coffee at noon while watching a rainstorm splash onto the track. To his credit and his coach's amazement, Jesse never once complained about missing lunches because he lacked the time to take a bus to and from the village. The athlete had been treated far worse by bigots in his native land.[8]

Jesse had been randomly assigned the first position on the inside of the track. Ordinarily, he would have been pleased to run in that position, but the rains and an earlier distance race had made that lane treacherous. The officials demonstrated that they were fairminded after all, moving all six competitors one lane to the outside.

Later, Jesse would reveal his thoughts at that moment. The pressure on him was tremendous. "I saw the finish line, and knew that ten seconds would climax the work of eight years," he said in his autobiography. "One mistake could ruin those eight years."

The crowd screamed encouragement to both Borchmeyer and Jesse, the two favorite athletes, but respectfully grew quiet as the six men threw down their trowels and eased into starting positions. At the signal, the six men sprang forward as if each had been propelled from starter Franz Miller's pistol. In a flash it was over. Jesse drew ahead of Metcalfe well before the halfway point and beat his rival by three feet. Osendarp settled for a bronze medal.

The crowd readily saw what Larry Snyder liked to say about Jesse's running style—there was no pounding and bruising of the cinders. He glided over the track like a croquet ball on grass. Applause for Jesse erupted when the officials concurred that his 10.3 time had tied world and Olympic records.[9]

Newspaper reporters pounded their typewriters, proclaiming Jesse to be a new Olympic hero. They used similes to refer to him as a black arrow, black bullet, black panther, true athletic genius, and whirlwind. "The first glimpse of Owens was astonishing," raved one British sportswriter.[10]

Jesse stood proudly on the victory stand. He bent to receive a laurel wreath and a medal. He accepted a symbolic tiny oak to plant. In film footage of the moment, he stands straight and erect and entirely self-possessed. Inwardly, he later revealed, he was controlling tears that threatened to run down his face. When he stepped down, his face was wreathed with smiles. At some point, Jesse glanced at Hitler's box and thought, most likely mistakenly, that he saw the dictator wave to him. The athlete gave a friendly wave back.

Jesse was astonished shortly thereafter when reporters approached him to ask if Hitler had snubbed him. Several newspapers ran a story claiming that Hitler refused to shake the black American's hand. These reporters neglected to inform readers that the dictator publicly shook no other hands that day in public—not even that of gold medalist Karl Hein, the hammer-thrower from Germany, who broke an Olympic record set twenty-four years previously.

Journalists of that era sometimes were prone to coloring a tale in broad, sometimes untrue strokes to titillate their readers and to give sports heroes near-mythic qualities. Many of these same reporters claimed that German officials, including starter Franz Miller, were unduly harsh on Jesse. However, not only was there no evidence to corroborate such charges, but Jesse himself always denied that the home country's athletes received any undeserved breaks from Miller, an excellent official.[11]

For some time after the Olympics, Jesse was to ignore the notion that he had been snubbed, quite possibly because Larry Snyder had urged him to avoid the controversy. He stayed neutral when reporters came around with leading questions.

"I haven't even thought about it," said Jesse. "I suppose Mr. Hitler is much too busy a man to stay out there forever. After all, he'd been there most of the day. Anyway, he did wave in my direction as he left the field and I sort of felt he was waving at me. I didn't bother about it one way or another."[12]

Years later, Jesse eventually told audiences that the dictator had in fact snubbed him. The tale has become a part of American legend—much like Babe Ruth's controversial pointing to the center field stands before hitting a home run to that spot during the 1932 World Series. In fact, Babe Ruth and Jesse Owens were alike in that both often spun slightly different versions of their key life events to suit audiences. Jesse's books contain versions of the same incidents that vary dramatically in the telling.

Nonetheless, if the Nazi Baldur von Schirach, leader of Hitler's youth movement can be believed, Hitler did snub Jesse. "The Americans should be ashamed of themselves, letting Negroes win their medals for them," said Hitler. "I shall not shake hands with this Negro."

According to Schirach, he and two other Nazi advisers kept pressure on the dictator, telling him that meeting the American track star was the sporting thing to do. "America will see the treatment of Jesse Owens as unfair," insisted Schirach. "He is an American citizen, and it's not for us to decide whom the Americans let compete. Besides, he's a friendly and educated man, a college student."

Hitler, for only the second time in Schirach's memory, exploded with fury. "Do you really think I will allow myself to be photographed shaking hands with a Negro?" he shouted.[13]

The discussion was over.

CHAPTER 9

Two Comrades

During the Olympics, Jesse couldn't afford to let the press entangle him in a political controversy. His third day of competition was his most demanding yet. In the morning, he was scheduled to run in two 200-meter qualifying heats, followed by the preliminary eliminations in the long jump.

Once again Jesse was flawless on the track. He established new world and Olympic records in the 200-meter events, this time with postings of 21.1 seconds in each heat. But while the other qualifiers, Mack Robinson (older brother of Jackie) and Bobby Packard went back to the village to rest, Jesse kept limber for the long jump event, fearing he might tear a muscle if his muscles were allowed to cool. Larry Snyder kept a close eye on him for signs of fatigue.[1]

Instead, Jesse lost focus and forgot temporarily the fundamentals that Snyder had taught him. In the qualifying trials for the long jump, Jesse botched his first two attempts, although the distance required was merely 23 feet 5 inches, and Jesse held the world record in that event.

The first poor jump was the result of an international misunderstanding. In the United States, at the time, competitors were allowed one practice jump to get accustomed to the take-off board. However, the Olympics in Germany allowed no free attempts. Without even removing his sweatsuit, Jesse took what he thought was a practice jump, his take-off foot partially hitting the foul line. When an official flourished a red flag, Jesse blinked in confusion, suddenly realizing that his half-hearted attempt had counted as a scratch.[2]

Jesse made no protest, but the call obviously shook his composure. He removed his sweatsuit for the second attempt, took off with perfect form, and leaped high across the sand. Jesse and a reporter from *The New York Times* covering the jump both thought he had qualified, but the German official disagreed. Once again, the red flag waved high. Perturbed, Jesse gave one of the judges a long, lingering look. After all the reports he had heard about the hatred of the Nazis for Jews and blacks, was it possible that this judge had blown the call on purpose to give a victory to the German hero Luz Long?[3]

Jesse's head raced with negative thoughts, disrupting the concentration he needed for a third jump. But he was too smart and talented an athlete to let his nerves get the best of him.

Hoping to see "some telltale sign of emotion," sportswriter Grantland Rice trained powerful binoculars on Jesse as the athlete got ready for his final attempt. If Jesse fouled again, his quest for a gold medal in this event was over. In spite of such maddening pressure, Rice reported, Jesse's face masked his thoughts. · Reasoning that he could not afford to gamble, Jesse had decided that conservative strategy was called for at the moment. Since qualifying was what was important, not a new world record, it wouldn't matter if the distance was somewhat less than Jesse usually jumped. What mattered was that he jump 23 feet 5 inches. In a brilliant piece of strategy, Jesse decided to take his jump from a point well before the foul line. He could worry about distance and setting world records once he got to the finals.

"Calmly he walked the sprint path in to the take-off board, then retraced his steps," wrote Rice. "Studying

German athlete Luz Long (left) and Owens became good friends, in spite of their different backgrounds.

the situation a moment, the American athlete 'anteloped' down that runway and took off at least a foot behind the required mark—but qualified!" [4]

Years later, Jesse wrote that he had gotten the strategy from Luz Long, but either the American was being generous to his German opponent, or the two men had compared strategies after the event. No one saw or heard them confer, and Jesse was in plain sight of Grantland Rice watching through field glasses. It was more likely that if they discussed the strategy at all, it was during a moment of socializing at the Olympics. Jesse said Long told him that he too had used the device of jumping a foot or so in front of the foul line to automatically qualify for a long-jump finals. [5]

During his stay in Berlin, Jesse found that he and his German antagonist Long had much in common. Like him, Long had a wife and had overcome the poverty of his parents through the outlet of athletics. Jesse was relieved to learn that his new friend harbored no racist notions about blacks.

"He didn't believe Hitler's Aryan supremacy statements and was disturbed by the military aggressiveness of the German dictator," Jesse later recalled. "Still, it was his country and he felt that if he didn't fight for it, he would be putting his wife and child in danger."[6]

Long was not the only German to treat Jesse respectfully. So many foreign athletes asked Jesse to pose with them that his face seemed perpetually frozen in a wide-open smile, Larry Snyder remembered. Athletes such as British wrestler Leslie Jeffers proudly kept photographs of themselves with Jesse as treasured keepsakes of the Games.[7]

The mutual affection of Jesse and Long was seen at the long jump finals. Long broke an Olympic record in his first jump. Jesse rushed over to congratulate him. The crowd in the vast concrete stadium applauded the feat and Jesse's display of sportmanship.[8] It looked as if Jesse had conceded the win to Long.

"Owens or no Owens, the Reich was doing all right," wrote Grantland Rice. "Hitler, watching from the 'royal' box, was preening his tailfeathers."[9]

The dictator did not have too long to preen. Jesse was being polite but had not given up. He followed Long and tied the record, landing 25 feet 9¾ inches from the starting line.

With the second jump, Jesse took over the event. He cleanly outdistanced Long, clearing 26 feet and making certain he did not foul.

Long exploded energetically on his own third and final try, but his toes grazed the starting line. He looked back miserably from the pit to see a red flag waving. Foul!

Jesse had the gold medal, but he was not satisfied. He often said the long jump was his "favorite" track event, "because at its best, it *is* like flying." What's more, he was dismayed by Long's foul, not wanting to read in the newspapers that he had won by virtue of a competitor's misfortune. "I decided I wasn't going to come down," Jesse was to later say. "I was going to stay up in the air forever."[10]

"Poised for his next attempt, Owens shot down the runway," said Rice, describing the event for readers in his own biography. "As he hurled himself through space, the Negro collegian seemed to be jumping clear out of Germany. The American cheering started while Jesse was airborne."

Many who saw Jesse's jump marveled that he was able to do it despite some major flaws in his technique. They wondered what miracles he might have been able to accomplish had his form been as impeccable as Luz Long's.[11]

The jump was clean. No flag waved. Jesse had a new world and Olympic record of 26 feet 5½ inches. Translated into metric terms, Jesse had jumped 8.06 meters—a record that track experts had claimed was out of human reach. The laurel wreath again adorned his head. He clutched his second gold medal and was given another oak sapling to plant when he returned home.[12]

When Jesse won the long jump, Luz Long ran to congratulate Jesse and to slap him on the back. The crowd cheered this display of unabashed camaraderie. They had witnessed perhaps the greatest one-on-one match in Olympic track-and-field history. Afterward, the two friends sipped coffee in the Olympic Village. Long seemed unconcerned and carefree, mystifying the American athlete.

"Don't you care?" Jesse demanded. "Don't you *really* care?"

Owens broke the Olympic record for the long jump while he competed in Berlin.

"I am here to struggle to win, Jesse," said Long. "But the first one I wish to beat is always *myself*."[13]

During this conversation, Long may have revealed to Jesse that Hitler himself had left his box to congratulate him out of sight of the prying American press—for indeed the dictator had done so. Getting the report second-hand from Long might explain why Jesse at first said he didn't feel snubbed by Hitler, only to reverse his story years later after Long's tragic death during World War II. Jesse might not have wanted to say anything disparaging about Hitler during the Olympics lest he give offense to Luz Long—even though an official Nazi publication had insulted Jesse and his Negro teammates, referring to them as "black auxiliaries," the equivalent of mercenaries. In the same vein, a top Nazi official referred to them as "non-humans," mentioning Jesse by name.[14]

Nonetheless, in spite of such hate-mongering, the most enduring photograph to come out of the 1936 Games was a shot of Jesse and Long, bodies nearly touching as they relax on the stadium's infield, engrossed in a friendly discussion. After the long jump finals, the two talked late into the night, overcoming barriers such as each's limited understanding of the other's language. The two athletes came away, as Jesse beautifully said, "with the priceless knowledge that the only bond worth anything between human beings is their humanness."[15]

Jesse actually stayed awake at some peril. Luz Long was finished competing; Jesse had the 200-meter run to qualify for in the morning. He was still tired upon awakening and felt less than his best. The weather remained cold, damp, and gloomy. Parts of the stadium floor were a quagmire. Rather than risk a pulled muscle, Jesse ran in a sweatshirt and shorts. He managed identical times of 21.3 seconds in two heats, while Mack Robinson had the best time with 21.1.[16]

The cheers of the crowd were reserved for Jesse after the event. In spite of Nazi propaganda that claimed Negroes were worthless, his graciousness, talent and good looks had charmed the German people. They chanted his name and thrust pieces of paper at him to sign.

Another athlete might have lost focus with so much attention, but Jesse somehow ignored all the clamor. He prepared himself mentally once again to race against Robinson for the finals of the 200-meter race. At the starting line, Jesse used his wonderful peripheral vision, keeping his eyes on the starter. Like a great base-runner studying a pitcher, Jesse had noticed that the starter invariably twitched his knees before firing the pistol. When the report came, he simultaneously came off the line like a falcon leaving its handler's arm.[17]

Robinson couldn't overcome that quick start. Jesse once again ran his best race, and he set both world and Olympic records for the 200-meter run with a time of 20.7 seconds. Winning the silver medal was Robinson with a time of 21.1 seconds.

With his third gold medal and symbolic young oak in hand, Jesse Owens stepped down from the podium to wild applause. "The world, including Adolf Hitler, was willing to concede that it had never seen a sprinter-jumper like Jesse Owens," exulted sportswriter Grantland Rice.

Perhaps the Americans offered the loudest cheers because Jesse supposedly had run his last Olympic race. They, like Jesse, knew that he was scheduled to run in only three events. The feat of earning three or more gold medals in a single Olympics had previously been accomplished by only one Olympian—Finland's Paavo Nurmi—who won four at the Paris Games in 1924. Even as Jesse donned dark glasses in an unsuccessful attempt to disguise himself from autograph-seekers, plans were being made without his knowledge to give him an opportunity to tie Nurmi for a fourth gold medal.

Behind the scenes, perhaps succombing to political pressure, American track coaches Dean Cromwell and Lawson Robertson decided to drop Sam Stoller and Marty Glickman—the only two Jewish athletes on the team—from the 400-meter relay event. Whether anti-Semitism was fully to blame, or whether the two coaches thought that breaking a commitment to the two dedicated Jewish athletes was necessary to put America's best runners in the event, has never been determined. Since Foy Draper—a runner who remained in the relay—was slower than either of the two excluded athletes, it's probable that the AOC had motives other than setting world records.

Glickman—who became a New York City-based broadcaster until his retirement in 1992—theorized that because Cromwell and Brundage were members of a pro-Nazi front organization, the America First Committee, the two had little or no sympathy for the plight of Jews. "The Germans had been terribly embarrassed by the success of our black athletes," Glickman told an interviewer. "To save the Germans from further embarrassment, [Cromwell and Brundage] didn't want to have the only two Jewish boys on the team win something, too."[18]

Relay team member Frank Wykoff, later a school superintendent in California, agreed that anti-Semitism was a factor. "I'm convinced it was the Jewish thing that was behind it," he once said. "Glickman and Stoller should have run."[19]

The AOC shamefully broke its commitment to the two Jewish athletes. In view of Hitler's anti-Jewish policies, which eventually led to the deaths of some 6 million Jews in concentration camps, the refusal of the American team to run its Jewish athletes was a despicable act of politics. Glickman and Stoller had trained as hard as all the other American athletes. They deserved a shot at bringing home a gold medal for their country. Ironically, in the end, even Germany allowed two Jewish athletes—fencer Helene Mayer and field hockey player Rudi Ball—to compete in the 1936 Games. Mayer and Ball captured silver medals in their respective events.[20]

Jesse himself thought that school loyalties, more than anti-Semitism, influenced the decision. He once said that Cromwell, a coach at the University of Southern California, likely wanted to give his own school a measure of glory by selecting two athletes (Draper and Wykoff) for the relay who had run for him at USC. "Probably if Glickman and Stoller had been from USC, they'd have run the relay," Jesse concluded.[21]

Whatever the reason, in the end, every member of the team brought over from the United States competed with the exception of Glickman, Stoller, and Eleanor Holm, a female swimmer who had been kicked off the team for training rules violations aboard the *Manhattan*.

When the two Jewish athletes were passed over, the new members of the 400-meter relay team became Jesse Owens and Ralph Metcalfe. Cromwell told the two black athletes a ridiculous story, assuring them that the Germans were rumored to have kept a secret contingent of runners under wraps for the event so that they could break the world record. At first, Jesse was delighted to get an opportunity for a fourth gold medal, saying he'd "sure hustle," when one American reporter talked to him.[22]

Later, according to Glickman's recollection, Jesse stood up to Cromwell and Robertson during a hastily called meeting of the track team.

"Look, Coach, I've had enough. I've already won three medals," Jesse said. "I don't want to run the relay. Let Marty and Sam run."

"Nothing doing, Jesse," Coach Robertson retorted. "You will run."[23]

Another controversy erupted just before the race. Dean Cromwell played favorites in the positioning of the athletes, giving former USC athlete Frank Wykoff the anchor slot instead of the more deserving Ralph Metcalfe. Metcalfe ran in the number-two position.

Jesse ran the first leg of the relay. His mission was to give the number-two man, Ralph Metcalfe, a commanding lead. Metcalfe took the baton and exploded in what may have been the best race of his life. Draper and Wykoff added to the lead, easily defeating the field. The story that the Germans had another string of super-runners to send in turned out to be hogwash; the team finished a very poor third. Once again, Jesse was involved in another world and Olympic record, finishing in 39.8 seconds.

According to stories Jesse later told, his teammates indicated that he should take the podium for the fourth time. Unselfishly he declined, insisting Ralph Metcalfe—the star of that brilliant relay performance—have an opportunity for the glory that had been denied him in three Olympic sprint races. In so doing, Jesse demonstrated to his teammates that he was, above all, a sportsman with a generous heart.

Also standing proudly was Foy Draper as he received a gold medal. Like Luz Long, his remaining days were few. The U.S. runner died in battle on foreign soil during World War II.[24]

All told at the Olympics—the last that would be held for twelve years because of World War II—Jesse competed fourteen times in three days, including the qualifying events and finals. He received four oak saplings for his efforts. He kept one, donating the others to his elementary school, high school, and college.[25]

Without brilliant performances by black athletes, the Germans would have rolled over the competition as they did in the majority of non-track-and-field events, such as gymnastics and fencing. One sportswriter summed up Jesse's brilliant performance in a single sentence: "Jesse was as smooth as the west wind."[26]

However, as if unwilling to give credit to the black Olympians, several sportswriters consciously or unconsciously denigrated the performances of black Americans. The so-called dean of American sportswriters, Grantland Rice, showed both ignorance and a reliance on stereotypes when he said: "almost lazily, and minus any show of extra effort, they have turned sport's greatest spectacles into the 'black parade of 1936.' "

With such a phrase, Rice apparently was able to convince himself and presumably some readers who shared his bias that Jesse's hard work, training, and attention to detail had been inconsequential. Rice also made sweeping assertions about African-Americans, telling his readers that black athletes "function best in intense heat."[27]

In a sense, such comments by America's best-known sportswriter of that era mirrored remarks made by Hitler to Albert Speer, head of Germany's Ministry for Armaments and War Production. "People whose antecedents came from the jungle were primitive," said the dictator, dismissing Jesse's accomplishments. "Their physiques were stronger than those of civilized whites. They represented unfair competition and hence must be excluded from future Games."[28]

When the Games were over, Hitler dropped all pretenses of civility. The oppression of Jews in Germany became a national obsession. Arms production increased as the dictator propelled his nation into the most horrific war ever waged. Before the Olympics, the Nazis had relieved the Jewish Captain Fürstner of his duties as organizer of the Olympic Village. At a banquet in honor of the new head of the village, the depressed Fürstner attended and fatally shot himself.[29]

Jesse came home a legend. He had triumphed over the world's best white competitors, and he had done so with good sportsmanship, grace, and courage. He had shown his wit and intelligence in interviews, and even the most jaded reporters had to take him seriously. None dared to quote him using stereotypical "darkie" dialect. In part because the U.S. Olympic team as a whole had lost in total points to Germany, sportswriters and the public became enamored with that team's greatest hero. In a few days time, Jesse had replaced Jim Thorpe as the greatest Olympian who ever lived in the minds of most Americans. Americans were no different from Hitler in that they loved to equate sporting success with national greatness.

Jesse's modesty and his patriotism won him many fans who otherwise had little interest in sports. Not all Olympians professed to love representing their nation the way Jesse kept saying that he did. For example, the great Finnish Olympian Paavo Nurmi rejected suggestions from reporters that he had brought great honor and glory to his country. "I ran for myself, never for Finland," he snapped. "At the Olympics, Paavo Nurmi mattered more than ever."[30]

Thousands of American bought tickets to movie theaters to see highlight newsreels of Jesse Owens's four medal-winning events. His name became known in almost every household. His handsome face was forever etched in the memories of every American. When he left the Olympic Village, newspaper reports wrote that Jesse's life course was set. Sadly, that was not to be. He would live to face trials that challenged him as much as or more than his brilliant performance in Berlin.

CHAPTER 10
The Price of Stardom

If Jesse Owens tried to take advantage of his name and fame, it should be noted that the Amateur Athletic Union took more than unfair advantage of Owens's new celebrity status after the 1936 Olympics.

Quick to punish an athlete who violated the code of an amateur by taking cash, the AAU in those days was not above exploiting a superstar for its own financial gain. Thus, when the U.S. Olympic team found itself in debt during the Olympics—in part because of lavish living by members of the American committee—it turned to Owens, Metcalfe, Wykoff, and other track heroes to bail it out. The AAU's fund-raising efforts on behalf of the Olympic team had been disappointing.

Owens was taken advantage of more than some other athletes because he found it hard to say no. When the Olympic 400-meter relay was over, Larry Snyder was celebrating with Owens in the team's locker room when he learned that the athlete had, in an unguarded moment, agreed to tour Europe as the AAU's star drawing card. Snyder was angry and stormed around the dressing room. With the pressure of the Olympics off Owens, Snyder had expected the sprinter would be able to relax and enjoy the balance of the Games. Instead, the AAU insisted that Owens leave the Village almost immediately so that he could participate in meaningless but profitable track meets across Europe. The angry coach cornered a representative of the AAU.

"You can't ask him to do that," barked Snyder. He

knew Owens was on the verge of burnout. He also knew that the AAU had not been candid with Owens about precisely what sort of grueling ordeal it was asking him to endure. In addition to a full slate of matches to be held in various cities that could only be reached by all-night train rides, Owens would have to submit to an endless round of banquets and parties. The athlete would be further ground down, forced to sign autographs, shake hands and socialize long into the night. There would be no sight-seeing except for what he could view from train and hotel windows.[1]

The representative stood his ground, saying that Owens had signed a contract, and he expected the athlete to be in Cologne, Germany, the next day to honor it. Because of Owens's great fame, promoters all across Europe had agreed to pay a bonus if the American star competed.[2]

The exhausted Owens already regretted his hasty acceptance of the AAU's request. His $8 had dwindled to mere pennies, and his desire to compete had been similarly depleted. He wanted to celebrate in America with his wife and daughter, and he missed them desperately. In part because they were financially strapped he wished to capitalize financially on his fame. A telegram from a U.S. promoter promised to pay him $25,000 for a two-week show-business stint on stage. (Jesse subsequently learned that the offer had been sent by a charlatan who had cruelly raised the athlete's hopes.) Larry Snyder unselfishly urged him to take the money. He told the athlete to get rich off his Olympic fame if he could, then finish his degree. He knew that Owens's dream was to coach at a black college, and he would need a degree to do so. (Coaching opportunities for blacks in white institutions simply did not exist in 1936 because of the racism in educational institutions.)[3]

While Owens was trying to collect his thoughts, a

breathless Ralph Metcalfe ran up to inform him that the AAU wanted the two of them to leave immediately for Cologne, not in the morning as first planned. Owens raced away to catch the train, while Albritton—who was not so rushed—went to the hotel room to pack his friend's clothes. He promised to catch a later train and deliver them. Owens couldn't even eat in the club car on the long ride. He couldn't afford even the most inexpensive meal.

"I was exhausted, in my soul as well as in my body," Owens later recalled. He had lost between ten and sixteen pounds. He hadn't had a day off in weeks, nor a long night's rest. He looked and felt fatigued.[4]

In the German city of Cologne, the first stop on the tour, the AAU scheduled Owens to race Olympic teammate Ralph Metcalfe in a 100-meter race. Once again his start was perfect, his feet treading as lightly as a fly's on cake. In contrast, Metcalfe came thundering down the track behind him, his feet pounding the track like sticks on a drum. Right before the finish line, Owens's old nemesis caught him, and Metcalfe was the winner.

In public, Owens was a gracious loser, warmly congratulating Metcalfe. He declared that Metcalfe's victory only went to show that he himself had had luck on his side back in Berlin. On any given day, athletes knew there always were talented competitors also willing to give their all, he said, adding that Metcalfe did not have four gold medals, but he had a champion's heart.[5]

But in private, to his Ohio State coach, Owens confided that he had found it impossible to take seriously so meaningless a race. "I just didn't care," said Owens. "I hope Ralph enjoyed winning that one. He can have it."

Larry Snyder knew that Jesse's statement reflected the runner's hurt and anger. The coach found it impressive that the battered Owens had come as close to a win as he had.

"Ralph is the second-best sprinter in the world, and was much fresher than Jesse, having taken part in only two events—the 100-meter and relay—instead of four," Snyder pointed out. "In addition to that, Ralph would have the added incentive of trying to beat the newly crowned world's champion."[6]

The next two weeks were a blur. According to Larry Snyder's account of the debacle in *The Saturday Evening Post*, the AAU required Owens to run in nine different races in eleven days. After a couple days off, Owens and the other Americans arrived in England for another meet. By this time, Snyder was more convinced than ever that Owens had been treated most unethically by the AAU. "They were using Jesse for bait," grumbled the coach.

Snyder thought that the AAU was treating America's best athletes like "trained seals." Owens, in particular, never received any respite from the autograph-seekers who besieged him everywhere.[7]

Even the mild-mannered Owens lost his temper finally, complaining that the AAU was making money hand over fist while the athletes, totally broke, couldn't even buy snacks or souvenirs.[8]

When the AAU demanded that Owens and Snyder head for yet another a meet in Sweden that had been arranged by a newspaper company, the coach bristled. He felt certain he was on safe legal grounds. Owens had signed no contract to come to Sweden, he reminded the official. After getting some advice from fellow track professionals, Snyder told Owens that the London meet would be his last.

Word of Snyder's decision reached Brundage, who warned the coach that the AAU would not take lightly this revolt by an amateur, not even one of Owens's status. Shortly thereafter, AAU treasurer Dan Ferris also made a blistering phone call to the Ohio State coach.

"What's all this about you and Jesse not going to Sweden?" demanded Ferris.

"Jesse's got a big chance," said Snyder calmly, defending the decision. "He's got a break that comes once in a lifetime and never comes at all to a lot of people. It's tough for a colored boy to make money at best. What kind of a friend would I be to stand in his way?"

Ferris erupted, saying that he had signed a contract with the Swedish promoters of the race. Now it was Snyder's turn to get angry, saying that Owens had never been told the trip to Sweden had to be made at the risk of losing his eligibility. He reminded Ferris that even the AAU had rules, and that one of those rules was that an amateur athlete had to sign a contract before he could break one.

"I'll have to suspend him," Ferris retorted.

"You can't suspend him in the Big Ten, because that's one organization you don't run," Snyder said before jamming the receiver down hard. "And listen, you're spending money on this call that could be spent on making up Olympic deficits."[9]

On the day that the Olympic closing ceremonies were held, Brundage and Ferris released a news bombshell that exploded back in America. They were suspending Owens for insubordination. As it turned out, had Owens attended the Swedish meet, he still would not have been off the hook. The AAU sent Owens's teammates to compete in nine more cities before permitting them to return home.

In 1936, the AAU's 600 voters punished Owens by awarding the James E. Sullivan Award for best amateur athlete to Olympic decathlon champion Glenn Morris. Owens would have been the first black to win the award.

Larry Snyder later said that in good conscience he couldn't let the AAU and IOC run roughshod over Owens. If the athlete didn't take these offers now, the coach said he could never forgive himself if someday Owens were penniless. Snyder stuck to his guns, even when Ohio State athletic director L. W. St. John put pressure on the coach to change his mind. St. John knew that Ohio State's track program was not nearly as attractive to fans without Jesse.[10]

Owens tried to give the American public an explanation for his actions. "I am turning professional because, first of all I'm busted and know the difficulties encountered by any member of my race in getting financial security," he said in a wire-service story the day after Brundage's announcement. "Secondly, because if I have money, I can help my race and perhaps become like Booker T. Washington."[11]

Owens and Snyder returned to America on the *Queen Mary*. This time Owens apparently suffered no seasickness, eating so much of the ship's cuisine that he gained back the weight that he had lost. While newspapers covered the controversy, the quiet but resolute Ruth Owens defended her husband to the press. "He should get the money while he can," said Ruth, who knew better than anyone else how tight the family's finances were. She also said that eventually she wanted her husband to finish his coursework at Ohio State.[12]

Ruth came to New York with Jesse's parents to greet the ship. In spite of Owens's fame, the city's hotels snubbed the family. Hotel managers informed them that they didn't cater to Negroes. A white Cleveland politician, in New York to greet Owens on behalf of the city, took control of the situation and found rooms for the family in a quality hotel. One black newspaper commented on the racist treatment accorded to a returning hero's kin. The elder Owenses must have reflected that things hadn't improved much since their sharecropper days.[13]

Nonetheless, the family was in good spirits as they boarded a Coast Guard ship to surprise Owens with a

Ruth Owens (right) and Jesse's parents waiting at a gala to welcome the athlete home.

visit before he docked in New York. "Am I proud of you!" his mother shouted at first sight of her son. She promptly tried to give him all the kisses he had missed since going away. Another surprise was waiting for Owens when he finally disembarked. His high school coach, Charles Riley, was there to clasp his hand.[14]

America gave Owens its warmest welcome. He was paraded through the streets of Cleveland and rewarded with gifts. By now a polished speaker, Owens was quoted in a Cleveland newspaper as he told an adoring audience that he promised to be a "worthy citizen." His hometown newspaper was no less proud of him. "Owens's fame is Cleveland's fame," boasted the Cleveland *Plain Dealer*. "To have produced such an athlete is a fine reputation for the city."[15]

The story of Owens's fight to overcome abject

Owens (near center) enjoying a welcome-home ceremony in Cleveland. His wife and mother are pictured on either side of him.

poverty was newsworthy. He told reporters how the family subsisted on carp given them by caring neighbors. "The Owenses are colored, so they do not have quite an even chance in this civilization," wrote one editorial writer. "They returned to poverty in the depression years and know what it is like to go hungry. . . . The Owenses are good people, churchgoers, good citizens unafraid of hard work. Jesse's mother is better than an average student of the Bible and trusts God completely. She and her husband have dignity and sensitiveness which no poverty, no bitter blows by life can overcome."[16]

From Cleveland, Owens returned to Columbus. Ohio State's faculty and students mobbed the new big man on campus. He was lauded and laden down with gifts. From Columbus, Jesse returned to New York to be feted with all the other members of the Olympic team.

Owens and Cleveland's mayor, Harold H. Burton (seated at right of Owens), taking part in the city's parade to congratulate the athlete on his success in the Olympic Games.

New York turned out in fine form to greet Owens. The crowd mobbed him, some reaching to touch his hand or arm. "He received a hero's welcome," reporter Gay Talese later wrote.

Fame acquired as quickly and sensationally as Jesse Owens obtained it has a magnetic quality. As soon as he won his fourth gold medal, people besieged the Olympic hero with offers—many of them related in some way to show business. An offer for $40,000 to join white minstrel-show entertainer Eddie Cantor turned out to be a hoax. Several other offers—including a chance to be in the movies—were also without substance. In a fit of gratitude, Owens had given black entertainer Bill "Bojangles" Robinson one of his four precious gold medals because Robinson's agent had said Owens would make $100,000 for appearing in a film.

"Some of [the offer makers] were as honest and fine as anybody I have ever met," said Larry Snyder, who acted as an unofficial adviser. But "there were plenty of others whose working tool, the chisel, was evident in every calculating phrase."[17]

Bojangles Robinson, for all his bombast, seemed above all others to have Owens's welfare at heart. Pushing sixty but in incredible physical shape because of his tap-dancing act, Robinson invited the Olympic hero to accompany him on tour. "People like Bill Robinson are proof that if a man works hard enough he can still make something of himself in a free country," Owens later declared.[18]

Owens briefly toured with a dance band, wearing a white tuxedo on the black nightclub circuit. The job was hardly safe. He witnessed knife fights and had to deal with crooked promoters. The schedule wore him out, and he contracted a strep throat infection in Richmond, Virginia. He got out when he saw that his talents and desires did not include singing or leading a band.

"I couldn't play an instrument. I'd just stand up front and announce the numbers," Owens later confessed. "They had me sing a little, but that was a horrible mistake. I can't carry a tune in a bucket."[19]

Because he had an amazing rags-to-riches story to tell, Owens was able to market himself on the lecture circuit. He spoke at banquet after banquet, traveling all over the country in his new Buick to speak to any group willing to meet his fee. He even took a large sum to deliver speeches all over America for the Republican candidate for president, Kansas Governor Alf Landon, but was unable to help him avoid a crushing defeat from the incumbent, Franklin Delano Roosevelt. ("Poorest race I ever ran," Owens later joked.)

His speaking skills brought him many thousands of dollars—more money in a year than his father made all his life—and he bought his parents a house on time payments and dressed Ruth in a style that highlighted her great beauty. Nonetheless, Ruth was a lonely woman. She went through a second pregnancy alone, but she rarely, if ever, complained.[20]

Owens spent money as fast as he made it. He missed running against competition and was happy when his agent set up a race in Cuba against that country's fastest amateur. But just before the competition was to transpire, Owens's old foe, the AAU, threatened to expel Conrado Rodriques if the athlete went through with his plans to race the banned Olympic hero, now a professional athlete. When the race fell through, the fast-talking agent arranged another deal. Owens would race a horse named Julio McCaw.

The promoters gave Jesse a 40-yard head start. He was to run 100 yards while the horse traveled 140.

Owens won the race and a purse of $2,000. At the time he laughed, thinking that he had found a source of easy money. But many years later he admitted that he had lost something very important by running against an animal—his self-respect.[21]

When he returned to the United States, Jesse contemplated returning to school—even though his athletic eligibility was gone. An older brother offered to give him his savings to finish college, but Owens didn't want to take the money. When Ruth informed him that another child was on the way, he made up his mind to quit and support his family of four.[22]

The only job America's hero of the moment could find was a poor-paying position as a recreation counselor and bathhouse attendant at a Cleveland playground. It paid $30 a week, $1560 a year. He had done better in college working all his part-time jobs.[23]

He hated the job and hated coming home to his dreary, two-room apartment. He was ready to jump at any opportunity. When a couple of fast-talking white promoters asked him if he weas interested in getting involved with a black baseball team, Owens snatched the opportunity without thinking twice.

That "opportunity" was the chance to race yet another horse prior to the start of every game. Perhaps conditioned to look at such freak contests as part of the norm, Owens accepted. While taking money for doing so didn't tear him apart all that much at the time, it did embarrass him looking back on his life in later years. "I was no longer a proud man who had won four Olympic gold medals," said Owens. "I was a spectacle, a freak."[24]

CHAPTER 11

Defeat and a Return to Glory

Jesse Owens's astonishing Olympic performance may have led to defeats later in life. He had won too easily and too often. Not only had the athlete given his best effort, but he had exceeded what he had once thought himself capable of achieving. Ever after, in his various business ventures, he had unrealistically high expectations of what he could do. He always hoped to recapture the glory he had known when the entire world was his in August 1936.

"Jesse only made one mistake in his life," his friend Mel Walker, an Ohio State teammate who had failed to make the Olympic team, once said to Ruth Owens. "He never lost when it really meant something."[1]

In part, Owens was unable to live the rest of his life unnoticed because the Olympics brought him press attention never before accorded a black amateur athlete. Other Olympians could put their gold medals into safe-deposit boxes and go on with their lives. The world would not let Jesse forget the glory days of Berlin. He had fame without fortune. He had won world acclaim but his privacy was lost forever.

"He tried to cash in on his Olympic heroics, but he could not make a living out of his sport, and off the track Owens was just one more black man trying to make it in a white man's country," wrote Chris Mead.[2]

Owens abruptly left the world of athletics in which his every moment was orchestrated by the Ohio State athletic department. He hoped to make his living in the fast world of business but he lacked the necessary experience and perhaps the aptitude. He liked to believe in the basic goodness of people, and he was not as sophisticated as he needed to be in his business dealings. While at Ohio State, the runner had always been a generous and easy mark, giving his friends the twenty-five watches he had won as trophies.[3]

Having come from an athletic program where his every appointment was set in advance and his every move was monitored, he tended to trust business associates to take care of financial matters. In 1938, for example, he found himself briefly in trouble with the Internal Revenue Service (IRS) after failing to file an income tax return in 1936. He and Ruth had to scramble to find the money to pay the bill.

Even worse, in 1939, Owens filed bankruptcy proceedings on a dry-cleaning business that had been established with other partners in his name and credit. Cleveland newspapers reported the failure, and his good name was damaged. Both his family and his parents had to move into less desirable living quarters.

In need of money, he returned to athletics. He began traveling with baseball's most famous black team, the Indianapolis Clowns. No baseball player himself, he earned his share of gate receipts by racing horses before games and local runners after games. Such promotional gimmicks filled the stands but failed to make him wealthy.[4]

Years later Owens revealed that beating a horse required less-than-admirable tactics. "There's no way that a man can *really* beat a horse, even over a hundred yards," he told reporter William O. Johnson, Jr. "The secret is—first, get a thoroughbred horse because they are the most nervous animals on earth. Then get the biggest gun you can and make sure the starter fires that big gun right by the nervous thoroughbred's ear. By the time the jockey gets the horse settled down, I could cover about fifty yards. Once that horse started galloping with twenty-, twenty-two-foot strides, man I'd have to go . . . to win in a hundred yards."[5]

Many of the ballgames were played before large audiences in the South, and Owens—who had been feted in some of the world's finest eating establishments—found himself eating sandwiches in his car again. Although restaurant owners knew his name and may have even cheered his Olympic exploits, they did not want to serve him. Even one of America's greatest black sports heroes could not live a life unaffected by racism.

During the winter Owens again left Ruth to tour with his own gaudily dressed basketball team, the Olympians. He put on running exhibitions at half-time, and after games he signed autographs seemingly without end. Once he explained to a reporter why he was so accommodating. "A little guy . . . is the one who keeps you alive," said Jesse. "He will come up and I don't care if I'm standing in a draft. I don't care if it is raining on my bare head, he will have my autograph. Also an hour of conversation if that is what he wants. I will not turn my back to him. I always got time for kids. That little guy is going to keep you in the public's eyes always."[6]

For several years after the Olympics Jesse kept on the road constantly but he had no savings to speak of. He saw little of his wife, daughters, and parents.

Owens received a serious blow in 1940. His mother passed away. She was worn out at sixty-four from a hard life of physical labor. Lost without her, Henry would soon die of a massive heart attack. Owens felt great despair. He had failed to show his parents that he could be a success in a field other than athletics.

"I couldn't escape the pain in [my mother's] eyes, the pain of seeing the world collapsing as my father had always known it would—of seeing the one son of hers she thought could break out reduced to spending his life paying off debts," Jesse wrote in *Blackthink*. Yet, even though he took financial responsibility for the cleaning business debts, throughout the remainder of his life he blamed the entire bankruptcy on his white partners, unable to face his own contributions to the failure.[7]

Jesse continued to scramble for money in undignified fashion, racing horses at county fairs and ball games and regretting his decision to drop out of college. At twenty-seven, he moved his family to Columbus and tried once again to resume his studies. Always a friend, Larry Snyder gave him a job assisting him with the track team. The money, however, was not enough. Owens had to open yet another dry-cleaning store. With the financial obligations that came with rearing his growing family of three daughters, Owens never really had a fair chance at getting his college degree. University officials had advised him during the mid-1930s to take his easiest classes first so that he could stay academically eligible for track. Unable to summon the time and patience required to pass his courses, Owens found his return to his alma mater to be disappointing. His cumulative average was significantly below passing, and his boyhood dream of earning a college diploma was gone.

Ohio State reluctantly dismissed Owens in December 1941. His inability to earn a degree embarrassed him. Years later, unable to face reality, he often stated that he had graduated from Ohio State. His failure to graduate was as much the university's fault as his own. With his full compliance, the school had exploited his athletic abilities to capitalize on his fame. The coaching staff failed to make certain that he made regular progress toward graduation.

Concurrent with Owens's leaving Ohio State, the United States formally declared war on Japan, Italy, and

Germany. Because he had three children at the start of the war, he was given a temporary deferment. His friend, Luz Long, was not so lucky. The German who loved Americans was killed on the battlefield by Americans while fighting for a government in which he did not believe.

The war changed Owens's conception of the glory that had been his during the Olympics. He realized that he had been naive to think that he personally had foiled Hitler's plans for domination of the Olympics. The newspapers had made it seem as "if I'd destroyed Hitler and his Aryan-supremacy, anti-Negro, anti-Jew viciousness," said Owens.[8]

As World War II raged, Owens's victories in athletic competition seemed insignificant to him compared to the damage the Nazis were inflicting with bombs, planes, and tanks. Owens knew he hadn't defeated Hitler. He'd merely impeded the dictator's grand plan. Hitler continued relentlessly to persecute Jews, to arm his people for war, and ultimately to cause the deaths of millions of human beings.

While Owens hated the Nazis, he nonetheless refused to call his friend Luz an enemy. "How could Luz Long . . . be an enemy after he came over and put his arm around my shoulder?" Owens kept asking himself.[9]

The war put Owens in the position once more of being useful to his country, enabling him to raise his self-esteem after his dream of getting a college degree was shattered. He earned a respectable living by conducting sports clinics and physical fitness seminars for the U.S. government's Civilian Defense Office from 1941 to 1942. With his good looks, exceptional speaking skills, and polish, he was a smash hit with kids of all ages. He still competed in silly exhibitions for quick money such as one-on-one races with his Olympic friend Helen Stephens, but at least his competition now was human.

In 1942, when the government began drafting even married men with children, Owens found managerial work in a Detroit automobile factory that had been converted to a defense plant. The job exempted him from service and left his weekends free for speaking engagements. After one promotion, he became director of Negro personnel for Ford, hiring and firing workers who built tanks and bombers for the war effort. He estimated that he hired some 50,000 black workers during his tenure with the company. The job required regular hours and gave him an opportunity to pay his bills and regain control of his finances.[11]

In spite of his job, Owens struggled financially, giving the bulk of his income to his creditors. It pained him to watch daughter Gloria growing up without the nice dresses and other frills that his workers on the assembly line could buy their daughters. "I watched Ruth . . . darning ragged hand-me-downs just as my mother had in Oakville twenty-five years before," recalled Owens. [12]

Owens's stay in Detroit coincided with horrific racial strife in the Motor City during 1943. Angered by wartime shortages and competition for housing by black and Polish blue-collar workers, the two ethnic groups engaged in a bloody, two-day skirmish that required National Guard action to quell the violence. Owens was appalled by photographs in the daily papers of African-Americans and whites alike dying in mob violence while the city burned. Because Owens was admired by both whites and blacks, Ford administrators tapped him to help improve public relations. The job lasted until October 1945, five months after the war in Europe ended and two months after Japan surrendered, ending World War II.[13]

During the late 1940s, three things brought Owens's name back before the American public. The first was that he began endorsing products for various companies. He was one of the first Olympic athletes to do so. He endorsed products such as automobiles, department-store chains, gasoline, tires, and beer—though he stopped plugging products with alcohol when his fans objected.

The second event was the much-publicized signing of baseball's first black baseball player, Jackie Robinson, to a Brooklyn Dodger minor-league contract in 1946. Robinson, an excellent player who made the parent club in 1947, said that if it had not been for the gains made by Joe Louis and Jesse Owens on behalf of black Americans, he would never have gotten an opportunity to play.[14]

The third event was the announcement that the Olympic Games would resume again in London in 1948. Because of the twelve-year hiatus, Owens's Olympics marks had stood since 1936, and his heroics were frequently discussed by the younger generation of track-and-field athletes who wanted to match or beat his records.

Stories about Owens appeared before and during the Games. When Fanny Blankers-Koen of the Netherlands won four gold medals in the London Games—the first woman to do so—reporters called her "the Jesse Owens of 1948." And in 1950, when the Associated Press took a poll asking people to name the greatest athlete of the half-century, Owens won by an overwhelming margin. Another poll of sportswriters named him one of the ten best black athletes of all time.[15]

To take advantage of Owens's restored popularity, sports promoter Abe Saperstein hired him to put on athletic exhibitions and to sign autographs during the late 1940s. Owens traveled with Saperstein's team, the

Harlem Globetrotters, on a European tour coinciding with the Summer Olympics held in rebuilt London. His fame alone was enough to attract crowds. He no longer had to demean himself by racing horses.

Leaving Saperstein at last, Owens moved to Chicago and started a public relations agency. His barnstorming had left him in terrific physical shape for a thirty-seven-year-old man. Even though he started smoking cigarettes in the late 1940s, Jesse still could defeat most young men in a race, running a 9.7-second 100-yard dash in 1950.[16]

In 1951, Owens returned to Berlin to visit Hitler's imposing sports stadium, which somehow had been spared bomb damage during World War II—although evidence of the destruction of war was present elsewhere in the city. Berlin was a troubled and divided city, hacked in 1945 into four occupation zones by the conquering Soviets, British, French, and Americans. In 1948, the Soviet Union blockaded all road, ship, and rail traffic between Berlin and the West, preventing food, fuel, and medicine from reaching the city. The United States had to airlift supplies to the beleaguered Berliners for two years.

Given the mood of the times, Owens's speech was sober but inspired. "Stand fast with us in the fight for freedom and democracy under the protection of Almighty God," he implored the Germans.[17]

During his visit to the Berlin stadium packed with 75,000 fans—some of whom had witnessed Owens's heroics in 1936—he again donned his Olympic sweatsuit. Although his hairline had receded, his belly was flat, and he looked the part of an Olympian. He loped around the track to salute the crowd, and the grin on his face was never broader as he basked in the shouts of approval and applause. He approached the box in which the mayor of West Berlin sat. The mayor grasped both Jesse's hands to make a point and said that Hitler's failure to shake the athlete's hand had been a travesty.[18]

One sad outcome of the fact that Owens had been thrust into the limelight as a defender of the American way of life was that the press and public felt justified in ignoring America's poor record on civil rights. The nation was in the midst of a most self-righteous period. The powerful House Committee on Un-American Activities was then denouncing and ruining the careers and lives of anyone who had shown sympathy with Communism. For example, a famous black actor named Paul Robeson was one of many talented and strong-opinioned Americans to become victims of the political witch-hunt.[19]

Owens, however, not only presented a non-threatening public persona, but his frequent speeches citing the virtues of patriotism, free enterprise, and the endless opportunities for blacks in America endeared him to white America. At the time, Owens was reluctant to speak against racial injustice, although he would become much more outspoken toward the end of his life. To show anger against social injustices in the 1950s, he knew, would turn white America against him. "I can get teed off. I am just as fallible as the next man . . . but I cannot show that I am teed off," he told an interviewer from *Sport* magazine.

In the end, both Robeson and Owens advanced the cause of civil rights, but in radically different ways. Robeson, although broken in health and spirit, was an inspiration for the militant blacks who came after him. During the 1960s, Robeson's "brilliant stand" against President Harry Truman and other political leaders had been praised by black religious leader Malcolm X. The actor had questioned "the intelligence of colored people fighting to defend a country that treated them with such open contempt and bestial brutality." The two were about to have a historic meeting when Malcolm X was assassinated.[20]

Owens, on the other hand, accomplished much by the fact that his heroics in Berlin had made him forever beloved by the American people. By virtue of becoming an American sports legend in the same sense as Babe Ruth, Notre Dame football coach Knute Rockne, Native American Olympic hero Jim Thorpe, and Olympic hurdler and professional golfer Mildred "Babe" Didrikson Zaharias, Owens's success heralded a time when black athletes routinely would be looked upon as heroes in America.

In a sense, Owens grew up with the country and the civil rights movement. As an old man he would become outspoken and even refer to himself as a "militant black." But during the 1950s and 1960s, in particular, he had the image of being a conservative, no-nonsense patriot. While such an image led radical blacks to say that Jesse had "sold out" to white America, his philosophy endeared him to moderate blacks as well as to conservative whites. If nothing else, Owens's contribution to civil rights was that he kept the rift between the two races from widening more than it did. *Reader's Digest*— the family magazine that often espouses the values of God and country—turned its pages over to Owens on occasion to express his opinions.

Owens sincerely believed for many years that optimism was the best policy. He chose to see advances in civil rights rather than to put emphasis on the failure of white America to give blacks all the equal opportunities coming to them under the U.S. Constitution. Perhaps because life had been so grim for him as a child in Alabama, he perceived that conditions for blacks in America were only getting better. Because he believed that true equality for the races was an ideal that would have to be achieved over a long period of time, he rejoiced with every black gain in civil rights, irritating true militants who agitated for rapid change.

During the Cold War between the United States and the Soviet Union, Jesse Owens's Olympic triumph in 1936 came more than ever to be regarded as a symbol of democracy's own triumph over totalitarian regimes. Because his speeches rang with the promise of America, he was perceived by the superpatriots of the day to be the ideal man of color. The Republicans, recalling how he once had campaigned on behalf of Alf Landon, showcased his support of their 1952 presidential candidate, Dwight D. "Ike" Eisenhower. Nonetheless, in spite of his reputation, Owens found himself floundering in the mid-1950s. He seemed to be running from banquet to banquet, telling the story of his Olympic victories over and over as if his life had somehow stopped having meaning after 1936.

A chance conversation with Martin Luther King, Jr., helped Owens get on track, the athlete wrote in his autobiography. "What *do* I do, Martin?" Jesse asked the civil rights leader. "It's too late for me to go back to school."

"All I can tell you is to build on what you know, what you love," responded King. "You can't run anymore, but isn't there something larger, something related to that part of your life, which you can use as an anchor for the new?"

Owens's solution was to teach. Lacking a degree, he could not coach at the high school or college level, but he did find a way to communicate his knowledge of athletics to children. In 1955, he obtained a political appointment with the Illinois Youth Commission, terming it "the most gratifying work I've ever done." The position lasted six years.

Always popular with the those he addressed in his speeches, Jesse found it particularly rewarding to be working with underprivileged children. In 1956, he or-

As he matured, Owens enjoyed working on programs for kids. He is pictured here with winners in the Jesse Owens Games.

ganized a "Junior Sports Jamboree" that served 1,800 kids between the ages of twelve and seventeen in 1956. He told *New York Times* reporter Gay Talese that he was trying to keep the students busy so that they would have no time to get into gang-related trouble.[21]

Another one of Owens's pet projects was Chicago's South Side Boys Club. He became a member of the board of directors, dedicated to offering programs that appealed to the predominantly black youth in the neighborhood.

Owens informed Talese, a young reporter destined for later fame as an author, that kids seemed to respond to "name" athletes such as himself. "The top athletes can keep the kids interested and out of trouble," he said. "They inspire kids, just as I was inspired by athletes when I was younger."[22]

In 1955, the State Department sent him on a good will mission to India on behalf of the United States. *Life* magazine accompanied him. "Owens was a practically perfect envoy in a country which has violently exaggerated ideas about the treatment of Negroes in the United States," observed the magazine's writer. Owens donated a check for more than a $1,000 to a Bombay youth organization to purchase athletic equipment.[23] He was the perfect diplomat, able to offer a positive perspective no matter how bleak things looked.

After a ruptured spinal disk literally paralyzed him on the golf course one day, making necessary an immediate operation to restore mobility, Owens saw only the bright side. "Too many people in this world don't get the opportunity to break their backs for success," he reasoned.

Nonetheless, he was only human. And he couldn't help feeling sorrow and regret as stronger, better-trained athletes began one by one to destroy his world and Olympic records. In 1960, at the Rome Olympics, the tall and lanky Ralph Boston shattered Jesse's treasured long-jump record with an Olympic and world record-setting leap of 26 feet 7¾ inches. Owens had attended, in part, because his former coach and mentor, Larry Snyder, was head of the Olympic squad.[24]

Always gracious, the perfect sportsman, Jesse told the Cleveland *Plain Dealer* that he was pleased to congratulate Boston on attaining such a "wonderful achievement." He also downplayed the importance of Boston's black skin. "People like Ralph keep the spirit of the Olympics strong," said Owens. "I was glad it was an admirable young kid who broke it—regardless of skin color. And I mean that."[25]

But he also was honest enough to admit that it hurt him to see his name figuratively scratched from the record book. "It's like having a pet dog for a long time," he said. "You get attached to it, and when it dies you miss it."[26]

However, Owens consoled himself with the knowledge that his own records certainly would have proved harder to break had he been able to race on modern tracks and if he had the advantage of modern training methods.

CHAPTER 12
The Elder Statesman

Although Owens's schedule kept him away from home for weeks and occasionally months, Ruth Owens made a home for the children. She accepted her husband's frequent and extended partings and tried to teach her three daughters to accept them, too. Whenever he came home, invariably bearing souvenirs, she had the girls greet him in their prettiest dresses.[1]

Ruth carved out a life of her own by helping out numerous charities. A private person, she worked anonymously, shunning the headlines that Owens always coveted. She decorated the numerous residences they shared through poor times and wealthy, painting walls or hanging wallpaper herself. She resisted becoming trendy in any way, even refusing to learn a black handshake that had become fashionable.[2]

"You're getting old," Owens sometimes shouted at her in exasperation when she spurned his suggestion they do something mildly daring.

"We're *both* getting old, Jesse," she always retorted. "The only difference between us is that *you* won't recognize it."[3]

Always faithful to her husband, Ruth Owens stoically concealed her hurt and disappointment over rumors of his philandering. "I've always maintained that [Jesse] would have to be a superhuman to do all the things that people say he does," she said, defending him from public attacks.

In private, Ruth was more direct with her husband.

"Do what you want to do, but respect me," she told him.[4]

The couple's daughters brought them much joy. The oldest daughter, Gloria, received an undergraduate degree from Ohio State, the first Owens to graduate from college. Gloria and the man she married, Malcolm Hemphill, gradually effected important changes in the large Chicago high school where they both worked. They were locally acclaimed as innovators after developing an educational model that helped many of their students to escape the ghetto. Malcolm in time became assistant principal of that school.[5]

Jesse and Ruth's daughter Marlene not only attended Ohio State, but was elected the first black homecoming queen in that school's history. In her triumph, she must have helped heal some of the pain her father felt over the racism he experienced at Ohio State.

The Owens's youngest daughter, Beverly, eloped while still a teenager, concerning both parents, but they relaxed as they came to know the young husband was a fine man.

In 1960, Jesse had an unexpected but touching reunion with his old high school coach, Charles Riley, with whom he had lost touch. A popular television show called *This Is Your Life*, which brought celebrities onto the show to be greeted by old friends and acquaintances, brought Owens to the show under some pretext. They arranged for his family and former Olympic teammates to be present and brought Coach Riley from a retirement home for the occasion. Jesse's love for the elderly coach was apparent to all who watched the show.[6]

Riley could barely see or hear, but he was obviously thrilled to be with Owens and his family again. It was the last time the two would meet. Riley failed to live out the year. Owens paid tribute again and again to the deceased coach, so ironically his mentor acquired fame in death that he had never known in life. "He was the first white man I really knew and, without ever trying, he proved to me beyond all doubt that a white man can understand and love a Negro," Owens once wrote. "I don't have to say how much I loved him."[7]

In his writings and public speeches, Owens again and again credited his wife and his high school coach for his success in life. Moreover, he was aware of his debt as an African-American to many successful blacks, famous and unknown. He believed that he was who he was because they were who they were.

"Not every man may have a Ruth or a Charles Riley, but every Negro has a Martin Luther King and a Joe Louis," Jesse wrote in his book *Blackthink*. "If the black man is owed a debt from the past, he owes a debt, too. He owes the men who have come before him, the ones who helped personally and the many more who helped him by standing up and not copping out when it counted. He owes it to them not to give in to violence and anger, owes it to everyone from Charles Drew, the person who set up the first U.S. blood bank even though his own 'black' blood would never be used, to Malcolm X, who finally came from hating all white men to hating only bigotry; from Crispus Attucks, the first man to die for the American Revolution at the Boston Massacre, to [poet] Langston Hughes, who always pleaded with his people to simply be eggs before they were colored eggs. He owes it to a lot of men, as yet unborn, who'll stand up in the future in a world that isn't gutted by hatred and rioting. He owes it to the best in himself."

Owens preached self-reliance, urging blacks not to take any white handouts until they had done everything possible to improve their situations on their own. His stands against food stamps and welfare were often noted by politicians. He blasted black slumlords who exploited their own people, and black drug dealers who encouraged young children to develop a dependence on narcotics. He criticized black leaders such as Adam Clayton Powell, a once-powerful and controversial black congressman from Harlem, charging that the politician had lost touch with the poor people in his district. Finally, he chided tennis champion Arthur Ashe for canceling an appointment to meet with ghetto children who were counting on him, because Ashe opted to accept a prestigious award instead.[8]

Owens was effective as a speaker and author because he illustrated his points with examples from his own life. He told how one of his daughters had been rejected by a light-skinned black suitor when he learned that both her grandparents had been dark-skinned. The incident, in part, inspired Owens to write thoughtfully on the then little-discussed issue of bigotry on the part of light-skinned blacks, and how light skin color had become a symbol of status in the black community.

"That some of us still love our own 'whiteys,' that *we* are prejudiced against Negroes, has long been a taboo subject among black people—above all when they're talking to whites," wrote Jesse Owens. "But we've got to come out with it, and then deal with it, because until Negroes can rid themselves of prejudices against Negroes, how . . . can they expect whites to act fair? . . .

"That doesn't mean you should stand still for bigotry. Fight it. Fight it for all your worth. But fight your *own* prejudice, too."[9]

Owens's activism never seemed to age him even as he reached his early fifties. He rarely seemed tired in public appearances, although he got by on four or five hours of sleep many nights. He was still athletic, but the ex-sprinter never adopted jogging for fitness. His two participatory sports were basketball against much younger men, and golf which he played with less than superstar success, thrilled when he could shoot in the high 70s and low 80s. He was striking in well-tailored clothes. His suits and shirts tended to be conservative, although his ties tended to be snappy.

As Owens approached his mid-fifties, however, his health failed him. He was no longer thin but stout, the result of eating his meals in hotels and banquet rooms. His body began to reflect the wear and tear he had extracted from it during his track-and-field career, but mostly it showed the effects of his addiction to cigarettes. He came down with pneumonia, checked out of one hospital against medical advice, and was rushed near death to another hospital.

Owens credited his wife with giving him the strength to fight back to health. "Fight, Jesse, fight . . . fight," Ruth whispered to the still figure in an oxygen tent.[10]

Owens once again defeated death, but he refused to stop smoking. The vice had gotten the best of him and would relentlessly destroy his health.

During the 1960s, Owens's views on civil rights were increasingly sought by groups that hired him to speak. Ruth Owens was a strong supporter of Martin Luther King, Jr., referring to him as an "angel." While Owens believed in the nonviolent teachings of Reverend King, the conservative in him had strong doubts about the wisdom of sit-ins and protests.

When in spite of her father's objections, his daughter Gloria took part in nonviolent protests in Chicago and Washington against the Vietnam War, it upset Owens until she and Ruth finally convinced him that civil disobedience was sometimes necessary to effect social change. As a result of their influence upon him, Jesse would come to repudiate some of his former beliefs and take a much stronger stand against racial injustice.[11]

At first he was reluctant to question the authority of the status quo, because he had personally prospered so much. "I can't forget my upbringing," he told a reporter. "I started at the bottom—and look at me now. I've got two homes, and I'm free to travel, and I know where my next meals are coming from. It's the Establishment that gave that to me. I tell the kids I talk to that the Establishment has been too good to me to knock it. I tell them that if they . . . *condemn* the system, then they have to have some ideas to *improve* the system."[12]

Martin Luther King's assassination on April 4, 1968, while supporting a Memphis civil sanitation workers' strike, made Owens distraught and also made him question his conservative views. "Brutal, unthinking force had been so effective," wrote the Olympian in one of his books. "We spend centuries slaving in manure to grow one man like this, and they snuff him out as if he were a dime-store candle, leaving four small children—no, four million children—fatherless."

Years later, when revelations about Martin Luther King's affairs with women surfaced, Owens defended him publicly and privately. In his book, *I Have Changed*, the Olympian attacked the FBI and its notorious director, J. Edgar Hoover, for running roughshod over King's civil rights. Hoover had authorized his agents to secretly spy on King. The FBI wiretapped the minister's hotel rooms to learn all that it could about his sex life.

"In a free society, is there any more immoral act than invading the rights of a citizen?" Owens demanded. He attacked cynics who gloated when King's womanizing surfaced, as if a strong man's weakness could excuse their own shortcomings and justify their cynicism. Owens, more than likely, anticipated correctly that his own personal life might be made public after his own death. Hoover also had authorized his agents to compile a large file on Owens that paid particular attention to the the Olympian's extramarital flings and financial problems. Thus, Owens's defense of King may be interpreted as defense of his own frailties where sex was concerned—and, more than likely—an apology for hurting his family with his own indiscretions.

"I know I'm no saint," wrote Jesse Owens. "Who is? A man doesn't live in this world sixty years without making mistakes. And I've had the opportunity to make some worse ones than most people. I'm not excusing them. . . . Even though a man tries to change, tries to grow . . . what gives him the very will to do it is the something inside himself that'll hopefully never change.

"I've done stupid things, and possibly they turned out to be cruel things. I'll regret them till the day I die. But to be brutally honest, there's a part of me that is still pure, a part I've never sold out."[13]

Owens insisted that society erred when it abandoned its heroes at the first evidence of human frailty. He asked his fans not to lose sight of all the good Martin Luther King had done. Owens noted that if they couldn't overlook King's human frailties, they should nevertheless remember his importance as the man who helped expose injustice against African-Americans in the United States.

CHAPTER 13

Stress and Strides

Every four years, Owens attended yet another Olympics in one official capacity or another. Each time the United States embraced new heroes and heroines in track-and-field.

In 1968, he attended the Mexico Olympics. He watched young African-American long jumper Bob Beamon sprint down the track, vault high into the air, and stay aloft for longer than even Owens in his prime. Thoughts of his own past glory must have flashed in Owens's mind as the officials measured the jump twice before proclaiming a new Olympic record of 29 feet $2\frac{1}{2}$ inches.

Perhaps recalling how Luz had so graciously extended his hand after losing the long jump, Owens raced over to be the first to congratulate Beamon. Owens told him that he was thrilled by the accomplishment, having believed that no human could ever jump that far. He demanded to know how the young man had leaped so far, according to Owens in his 1972 book, *I Have Changed.*

"What can I tell *you*, Jesse?" he said, as if mystified himself by what he had done. "The mental, physical, emotional, who knows what? It all came together, man! You try for years. *You* know. You try and try. Then one day—for one swinging minute—I guess it all just works."

Owens returned home, certain that he would never see another long jump that impressive in his lifetime.

He wrote an open letter to Bob Beamon to thank him for achieving a truly wonderful accomplishment.

"That incredible record-breaking jump of yours at the '68 Olympics was the most thrilling athletic feat I've ever witnessed, not just because I love to see a good man do his best, but because you jumped better than your best—better than you were actually 'capable' of. *That* kind of miracle happens only once or twice in a lifetime. It happened to me, too."[1]

Like the 1936 Olympic Games, the 1968 Games became newsworthy because of the part politics played in them. Once again, Owens found himself swept up in political events. This time many of the American black Olympians, supported by several white teammates, decided to use the Olympics as a forum to protest the treatment of African-Americans in the United States. Before the Games, rumors that blacks who won their events planned to protest the awards ceremony began to surface. Owens put himself directly into the controversy when he wrote a pre-Olympics article for *TV Guide*, begging African-Americans not to "embarrass the United States in so conspicuous a world arena."

Newspaper and magazine reporters flocked to interview the hero of the 1936 Olympics. "I deplore the use of the Olympic Games for political aggrandizement," Jesse told them.[2]

While the 1968 Olympics conspicuously pitted blacks versus white injustice, another rift was also present. The Games pitted conservative Owens against liberal young black Olympic sprinters Tommie Smith and John Carlos, students from San Jose State who had studied under outspoken African-American sociologist Harry Edwards.

Owens took his usual conservative view, insisting that individual achievement by blacks would eventually defeat racism in the United States. But Smith and Carlos—backed by nationally known militants H. Rap Brown and Stokely Carmichael—believed that it was the duty of black achievers to combat racism wherever it existed at all costs. There was no room for compromise. Each side felt it was in the right. Both equated compromise with backing down, and neither would do that.

Smith and Carlos believed in symbolic civil disobedience. One of the symbols of protest was a clenched black fist. When the two sprinters won gold and bronze medals respectively in the 200 meters—with Smith establishing a world and Olympic record time of 19.83—they extended black-gloved hands over their heads during the playing of the U.S. national anthem.

Owens said that the symbolic gesture was repugnant to him personally. He said that blacks would not truly be free until they were economically independent. "The black fist is a meaningless symbol," Jesse told a reporter. "When you open it, you have nothing but fingers—weak empty fingers. The only time the black fist has significance is when there's money inside. That's where the power lies."[3]

Ironically, the same International and U.S. Olympic Committees that had treated Jesse less than fairly in 1936 now came to ask his help in smoothing over Smith and Carlos' protest. After IOC President Avery Brundage—Owens's old adversary—heard Owens on a radio program pleading with blacks not to boycott the Games for political purposes, he had written Owens a long letter praising his views. Back in 1936, the two could never have foreseen that someday they would be allies. Owens asked several athletes to reconsider their decision to boycott. The boycott turned out to have limited success, supported by few stars with the exception of UCLA basketball star Kareem Abdul-Jabbar (known then as Lou Alcindor).

Following the protest, Owens went as a representative of IOC President Brundage to ask Smith and Carlos to recant their actions. Jesse met with them and Harold Connolly, a white hammer-thrower, who fared poorly in 1968, but who had won a gold medal for the United States in the event during the 1956 Games. Connolly wanted to persuade the African-Americans to symbolically dip the American flag to protest racism, but Jesse convinced him that to do so was to dishonor Americans who had died in battle while flying those colors.

That confrontation was Owens's only victory. With Connolly's encouragement, Carlos rebuffed Owens's attempts to get an apology for Brundage. "It don't make no difference what I say or do," Carlos said. "I'm lower than dirt, man. I'm black."[4]

Connolly's jeering in the background annoyed Owens. He asked Carlos to explain why he was so dependent on a white man like Connolly when he was otherwise rejecting the white society as a whole. Owens had apparently forgotten how Larry Snyder had influenced his own political views about Olympic competition in 1936.

The meeting ended in a stalemate. The young black athletes wanted the world to hear their views and would not compromise. Neither would Brundage and the IOC. Smith and Carlos were ordered home from the Village. It would be many years before even mainstream magazines such as *Sports Illustrated* would applaud their protest as a heroic gesture, seeing it as a milestone in civil rights progress.

Owens at the time was disconsolate. When Carlos rejected his advice, Owens was certain that everything he had tried to do to help black-white relations was for naught.

Paradoxically, while the militant athletes snubbed him, he was as well known and as beloved by Olympic fans as he had been at any time since 1936. Owens and other well-known Olympians had their own box of honor, provided in 1968 by the Mexican government. Owens could barely move in the stadium without escorts to keep back throngs of autograph-seeking fans.

Deeply troubled, Jesse wrote a book called *Blackthink* in collaboration with Paul Neimark, that took issue with "pro-Negro, anti-white bigotry" in America. He hoped that the book would reverse the image of black athletes which he believed had been tarnished in Mexico City. As much as anything, Jesse had been stung by strong criticism leveled against him by Harry Edwards, who referred to the old Olympian as an "Uncle Tom," a pejorative reference to the faithful old slave terrorized by a brutal master named Simon Legree in Harriet Beecher Stowe's 1851 novel, *Uncle Tom's Cabin.*[5]

In some ways *Blackthink* was simplistic. Jesse saw athletics as a way for blacks to escape the ghetto, failing to see that only a small percentage of athletes are good enough to become Olympians or professional ballplayers—let alone superathletes like Jesse Owens.

Owens, who was away from his wife and daughters so often, also failed to consider the needs of African-American women. "Sports represent the American dream," said Owens. "If a boy can't grow up and make it there, he can't make it anywhere."

African-American leaders attacked Owens when they read his book. They were upset by his contention that any black who failed to succeed in the American land of opportunity had "chosen to fail."[6]

But Owens's book is nothing if not passionate. He felt that he had something urgent to say. His message was that love would win over hate and that tyranny by black extremists was as inexcusable as tyranny imposed by the American Nazi Party or the Ku Klux Klan. "Hate is a tricky thing," Owens said in *Blackthink.* "It's malignant. The black militants I've known all ended up hating much more than the white man—their own women, families, closest friends. For, deep down, they *must* hate everyone."

He attacked anti-Semitism on the part of certain black leaders, saying that the Jewish race had done something that the radical African-Americans had been unable to do. "They've overcome," wrote Owens. "That doesn't sit well when you've copped out yourself."[7]

Owens stated his opposition to violence as a solution. He said he feared that racist blacks, like racist white supremacist organizations, were conditioning other people to think that violence is a solution to social problems. He insisted that it was unrealistic for blacks or whites to look for quick fixes to racial problems. He said the crisis between whites and blacks was as much a people problem as it was a racial problem. "Violence, poverty, prejudice, all the rest—these aren't Negro problems," contended Owens. "These are *people's* problems.

Mainly, however, the book was a reaffirmation of Owens's life, although it was justifiably attacked by some readers for its exaggerations and inaccuracies. He reminded Edwards that he too had been scarred by racism. He wrote that he had persevered and succeeded in spite of being shunned, insulted, ridiculed and refused service. "You can never escape scars so ugly and deep they still hurt like open wounds," wrote Owens. "But there are some pieces of yourself that you *must* keep whole."

Significantly, Jesse's own problems with poverty began to disappear during the late 1960s. Although slowed by serious tax problems with the Internal Revenue Service, his publication of *Blackthink* and his strong anti-militant stand at the Olympics led to opportunities to endorse products, and he would remain financially successful to the end of his days. He bought a summer home in Michigan for family reunions and accumulated a modest nest egg that would take care of Ruth comfortably after he was gone.

Other teammates of his from the 1936 Olympics had also prospered. His boyhood friend, David Albritton, was a bank executive and a member of the Ohio State Legislature. Ralph Metcalfe was a powerful politician in Chicago. Marty Glickman overcame anti-Semitism to become a much-beloved announcer—the voice of the New York Giants and New York Jets.[8]

Nonetheless, the banquets, speeches, and endorsements hardly made the Owenses wealthy by the current standards of a Michael Jordan or Carl Lewis. One writer estimated in 1971 that Owens earned in the neighborhood of $75,000 annually for his work. The cost of such comfort in human terms was tremendous, however. Well over half a year was spent away from Ruth and in the company of strangers. At a time when many couples grow closer, Ruth continued to endure her husband's comings and goings, knowing that whatever drove him would drive him to his last breath. He was not one to cultivate a lawn or even sit on the porch like his father had. He was, in effect, a showman, never so happy as when seeing hero worship in the eyes of his audience.[9]

In spite of his success as a public speaker, Owens never quite got used to addressing hordes of strangers. He continued to smoke cigarettes as a way to calm his nerves. "I *always* have these . . . butterflies when I talk," he told reporter William O. Johnson, Jr., prior to a Jaycees' banquet in Binghamton, New York. "Wouldn't you think I'd get over it?"[10]

Owens's face was known almost everywhere he went just as it had been back in 1936. Television documentaries began running footage of his Olympic feats, winning him many young fans and rekindling the passions of old ones. One film, *Jesse Owens Returns to Berlin*, contained touching footage of the athlete's reunion with Karl Long, son of the German Olympian buried in a grave on North African soil.

In addition, he represented the United States once again in an official capacity after Republican Richard M. Nixon became president in 1968, going to West Africa as a goodwill ambassador. As a measure of his success, officials in Abidjan, the Ivory Coast capital, named a street in Owens's honor.[11]

Even as he aged, Owens seemed willing to do anything to please his fans. He had a reputation for doing anything they requested—even if it took him away even longer from his patient wife.

"You could be ever so tired, but the public is a funny thing," Owens told a *Sport* magazine interviewer. "The public will not tolerate nonsense from anyone it has taken to its bosom. The public has made you, even though you have won something on your own. It is the public which seeks you out. The public will not stand for prima donnas for long. There are many times now when I don't feel like doing something—signing autographs or speaking with an audience or having dinner with people I have never seen—but the public is not interested in explanations. You got to smile. You must. The moment you begin to think you are an ordinary human being with ordinary human being rights, then the public does not want you any longer. If you are ordinary then the public can no longer look up to you."

Some writers ridiculed Owens for putting on his best face in public. *Sports Illustrated* reporter William O. Johnson, Jr., wrote a scathing account of Owens's public persona, dismissing him as a "super-combination of nineteenth-century spellbinder and twentieth-century plastic PR [public relations] man."

Nonetheless, Johnson himself observed that Owens was always cheerful and solicitous with young people, giving every last one his signature, his smile, and his voice. "Your name's Darlene? How are you, Darlene, ol' buddy?" he would say. "Mike? How are you, Mike, ol' buddy, you gonna be a runner?"[12]

Owens always was at his best and most comfortable with children. He kept an award given him by some children in a place of honor next to his remaining Olympic gold medals. At one Philadelphia track meet, he encouraged young Carl Lewis, who would one day himself become another great American Olympian. Owens perfected a repertoire of speeches on topics such as motivation and values, religion, and patriotism.[13]

"Awards become tarnished and diplomas fade," he reminded young people at the banquets he attended as guest speaker. "Gold turns green, and ink turns gray and you cannot *read* what is upon that diploma or upon that badge. Championships are mythical things. They have no permanence. What is a gold medal? It is but a trinket, a bauble. What counts, my friends, are the *realities* of life: the fact of competition and, yes, the great and good friends you make."

CHAPTER 14

Approaching the Finish Line

One evening Owens attended a civil rights gathering at the home of a wealthy businessman. Despite the nature of the evening, he and Ruth were the only blacks invited. Owens was bewildered, wondering why he had been so singled out.

"You'll just never quite understand it, will you?" Ruth said to him.

"What, honey?" he replied.

"That the white world will do things for Jesse Owens that it simply will not do—even when it should—for anybody else."

The simple truth in her statement shocked and upset him. Later that evening, a white businessman at the party touched a match to a stick of dynamite when he gave Owens's *Blackthink* a back-handed compliment.

"You exposed those militants the way it needed to be done," said the benefactor. "Good going."

"I'm afraid I can't accept the compliment," Owens said, his voice gone frigid and tight. "I'm a militant too."[1]

He and Ruth left the party early. Owens knew that he couldn't convince the man that being militant and being violent were not one and the same. What he wanted was social change and the chance for blacks to have the equal protection under the law that the Constitution guarantees them.

"Mr. President—let my people go," he wrote in an open letter to President Richard M. Nixon in 1972, requesting a pardon for Eldridge Cleaver, a founder of the Black Panthers and author of *Soul on Ice,* who then was living in exile in Algeria. Although he was a lifelong Republican, Owens's sense of justice made him wonder aloud how a president who could find a way to open a dialogue with Red China could not find a way to speak with black militants such as Cleaver and Angela Davis. "They're *your* people, too. They're the underdog. They're human beings."[2]

As he became an elder statesman, Owens began to sound blunter in his public pronouncements. He contended in his 1972 book, *I Have Changed,* that blacks have more difficulties achieving success than whites do because of societal racism, repudiating what he himself had said about black failures a few years earlier.

His philosophy, in some ways, was the same. He advised young blacks to work within the system instead of rebelling. "They *did* have a chance" to succeed, he said, "if only they'd work twice as hard and turn the other cheek when the first one was maybe raw and open to the bone."[3]

He dreamed of uniting not only the black and white races, but of conceiving "a fresh position" that might join both black moderates and militants in a common cause. He also wanted to help America restore its national pride.

"Communication is at an all-time dangerous low," Owens wrote in *I Have Changed.* "Whites feel guilty about blacks, blacks are bitter toward whites. Parents are resentful against kids, kids mistrustful of anyone over thirty. Women against men. Homosexuals against straights. Consumers against manufacturers and on and on. . . . Only in this ironic incredible mass-communications center which is America do we have so much talk about all of it and so little real *communicating.*"

Although it was painful, he admitted the possibility

that his ideas for changing humankind not only wouldn't succeed, but might fail dismally. He admitted, indirectly, that many blacks simply ignored his message, refusing to take advice from a man who had first won fame with his legs instead of his intellect. The knowledge hurt, and Owens admitted feeling jealous of those men that the black community did embrace. "What did Malcolm X and Eldridge Cleaver have that I didn't have?" he asked rhetorically in *I Have Changed.*

In his last years, Owens continued to effect social change whenever he could. In his role as a consultant to Major League Baseball's American League, he quietly let it be known that he thought it unconscionable that the big leagues had never had a black manager. In his quiet way, he took great pride in the fact that it was the American League which hired the first black manager, Frank Robinson of Owens's hometown Cleveland Indians, in 1975.

No longer a young man, Owens cultivated a thin moustache—oddly trimmed in the center—as his remaining hair dwindled. Dental work had repaired some irregularities and given him a toothier smile than ever. But his smile was all that remained of his boyish look. His eyes were set in deep hollows, and his smoking habit had stolen the bloom from his complexion. His face was spotted with the marks of age.

Yet, in a way, he was still an athlete, keeping a schedule as he fast approached sixty that would have flattened most people in their thirties. He claimed to travel some 500,000 air miles per year.

"In the space of less than seven days, I attended a track meet in Boston, flew from there to Bowling Green [Ohio] for the National Jaycees, then to Rochester for the blind, Buffalo for another track meet, New York to shoot a film called *The Black Athlete,* Miami for Ford Motor Company, back up to New York for forty-five minutes to deliver a speech, then into L.A. for another the same night," he once said.[4]

His relationships with his daughters, occasionally stormy when their modern, sometimes radical views clashed with his Republican conservatism, began to mellow as they themselves prospered. "Your differences have shown me the incomparable value and beauty of human differences better than all else," he said, in a special letter to them printed in *I Have Changed*.

One day, when his daughters had come with their families to his home for a relaxing weekend, he searched their faces and wished he could see clear to their hearts.

"I wondered if I had shown them all the love I had in *my* heart for *them*," he mused. "Or had I let our petty disagreements and my busyness get the best of our relationships. Did I want to play the unflawed father figure forever?"[5]

Inspired by his daughters and their husbands, Owens took up such causes as equal housing, angrily rebutting white stereotypes that blacks "always" let their properties get run down. "Let's be brutally honest," he said in *I Have Changed*. "If more blacks than whites *do* let their property go to hell, isn't it because *all* blacks were made to live *in* hell in this country for a hundred and fifty years? Humanity—or inhumanity—is always at the bottom of every 'issue.' "

He took shots from reviewers who thought that he was naive to believe that positive thinking was enough to propel blacks out of the ghetto. He conceded that he might indeed be naive, but didn't his own example count for something? He urged young blacks to make the most of their own lives, and to advance themselves by getting an education since so few of them could achieve success in athletics to become another Kareem Abdul-Jabbar, Joe Louis, or Jesse Owens.

Though he never graduated from Ohio State University, Owens received an honorary degree from that college in 1972.

In *I Have Changed*, Jesse printed verbatim a letter from a twenty-three-year-old, black Vietnam War veteran to back his claim that a positive attitude, when combined with education and plain hard work, could propel people out of lives of poverty.

"We poor blacks can advance in spite of any ghetto," wrote the young man. "Both of my parents dropped out of grammar school, but I defied the gangs and finished [high school]. Now, by having served in Vietnam, I shall enter Fisk University under the GI Bill of Education this fall.

"Anyone who wishes may read, read, read and read at no cost at the library . . . and improve his grammar as I am still trying to do. Good grades, and especially the GI Bill of Education for men or women vets, will take care of any college expenses. It can be done—I know."[6]

Owens's own frustration at his inability to earn a college degree ended in 1972. Ohio State acknowledged him at graduation ceremonies that year by presenting him with an honorary doctor of athletic arts degree.

That award signified that Owens's accomplishments in life were worthy of the highest honor Ohio State could bestow. That an African-American athlete could be so honored would have been inconceivable to Jesse Owens and his parents back when he was a Buckeye undergraduate. Times *had* changed and Owens's alma mater was not only trying to make amends for the past, but also was trying to honor one of its favorite sons.

CHAPTER 15

End of the Race

Even with enough money to retire, Jesse Owens refused to leave public life. Although Ruth persuaded him to move to the gentler climate of Arizona, and he became a devoted husband as he grew older, Owens kept moving as he always had. He had little patience for people his own age who refused to get involved with the world's problems.

"What can *I* do?" an old acquaintance whined to him one day. "I mean, how many years have I got left, Jesse?"

"Man, that's just the point," Owens retorted. "I ask myself how many years I've got left and that's what makes me want to get these things done."

Perhaps the greatest fear expressed in Owens's writings was that he'd someday grow old and useless. "How can a man like me ever prepare for being old?" he asked rhetorically. He concluded that he preferred a relatively early death to feeble old age, wishing only that he might still be busy and feel needed when his time came.[1]

Owens often said that it was his mission during his remaining years to "showcase" the good he found all around him. Though he was sarcastically called "a professional good example" by *Sports Illustrated* writer William O. Johnson, Jr., Owens lived by a simple but noble code: "No matter how much bad there is, the very best way to get rid of it is *by exposing the good*," Jesse maintained. "Don't just hack away at the roots of evil.

They go all the way to China. Plant next to prejudice another tree that grows so big and high that discrimination has to wither and die."[2]

Owens frequently talked about life through the metaphor of track. He found that it was a mistake to try to take life as a sprint as he had done earlier in his life. The race was too long to take it at a dead run. No one had that kind of strength and endurance, not even Jesse Owens. Life, he had learned, is more like a marathon; in his words, it's "a long, long, long-distance race over hills and through valleys, sometimes even with stops along the way, and it's how you run that marathon, not how soon you get to the finish line, that matters. Because there really is no finish line. As long as you live, there's another hill, another valley."[3]

Trying to be brutally honest with himself and his millions of fans, he downplayed who he was and what he had been. "I'm no iconoclast, no innovator, no philosopher," said Owens. "I'm only someone who had a unique pair of legs and maybe a little extra drive to go with them." He referred to himself as "an essentially ordinary man trying to make sense of the experiences of my life and what's going on around me."[4]

But he was proud of what he had accomplished, and no matter what problems and failures he had in his life, no one could ever take away his near-miraculous performance at the Berlin Olympics or close the doors on black athletes that he himself had opened. The son of a sharecropper gave credit to his Maker for much of his good fortune. "Miracles happen," he said. "You might have to strive almost your whole life for just a few seconds of one. But it's worth it. Man, how it's worth it."[5]

Owens believed that no matter how nice it was to set records, they were unimportant in the end. For him, what was important was that he had participated, dreamed, and done his best. "What counts is that day-

Even as he aged, Owens always kept his winning smile.

in, day-out exercise of your character, your guts, your free will, which makes the you that hurts and the you that's joy and the you that's tired and the you that won't quit . . . all come together," he said in *I Have Changed.*

He rejoiced whenever adults stopped him on the street to say that a speech he had given many years earlier had an impact on their lives. "I think to myself, that man probably has children of his own now," Owens once told a reporter. "And maybe, *maybe* he remembers a specific point I made, or perhaps two points I made. And maybe he is passing those points on to his own son just as I said them. And then I think . . . that's immortality. You are immortal if your ideas are being passed on from a father to a son and to his son and on and on."[6]

Owens went home to Alabama one final time in 1979. He received an award for patriotism in a service held in Decatur, a few scant miles from the farm his parents had sharecropped.[7]

Toward the end of his life, Owens moved to Phoenix at his wife's insistence, hoping that the Arizona climate might improve his health. In Chicago he had been experiencing chest colds that would not go away, and she feared that yet another bout of pneumonia would kill him. The least exertion, even getting off a sofa to walk into another room, tired him and made him gasp.[8]

He watched some of his friends die, including his old rival, Ralph Metcalfe, who died of heart failure.[9] Another pal and fellow-legend, Joe Louis, also began to deteriorate. For a time the boxer found treatment in the mental ward of a Denver hospital for veterans. Suffering a heart attack and cerebral hemorrhage in 1977, he lost the ability to use his legs and was confined to a wheelchair for the rest of his days. The irony of America's boxing hero down on his luck disturbed Jesse. He wondered why Louis's fans weren't forming lines to help a champion in trouble. "Joe Louis is down," he wrote in *I Have Changed*. "Joe, the sweetest, most beautiful thing you ever had, America, is hurt. Hurt *bad*. Mercifully, wealthy singer Frank Sinatra—a longtime friend of the champion—stepped forward to pay Louis's hospital bills.[10]

Jesse had long had a premonition that like his parents, he'd not live to be ninety. "I doubt very much that I will," he accurately predicted in 1970, "because I've lived these fifty-seven so hard."[11]

His longtime habit of smoking caught up with him at last late in 1979. Unable to quit he had switched in his mid-sixties to a pipe, but the damage to his lungs and heart already had been done. His lungs, already weakened by his boyhood bouts of pneumonia, had become spotted with black soot stains and the yellow, patchy growths of cancer. Doctors gave him but a few months to live.

Courageous to the end, Owens kept involved in American athletics. He waged an impassioned battle to convince President Jimmy Carter to resist his inclination to boycott the 1980 Olympic Games in Moscow as a protest against Soviet aggression in Afghanistan. He lost that final battle, although his death preceded Carter's announcement of a boycott. Although he was inclined to support the president's decision, Owens offered a suggestion that unfortunately was ignored. He proposed that American athletes compete in Moscow as individuals, not as a nation, so that their years of hard work would not be sacrificed in the name of politics. "The road to the Olympics doesn't lead to Moscow," said Owens. "The road to the Olympics leads, in the end, to the best within us."[12]

Those were his last public words. Cancer destroyed his once magnificent body. The end was difficult. His ruined lungs kept him coughing, making both breathing and sleeping almost impossible. All his doctors in a Tucson hospital could do was try to make his end a little less painful. His mind remained clear, however, until two days before his death. He died at the age of sixty-six on March 31, 1980. Another legendary African-American died soon after him. On April 12, 1981, Joe Louis suffered a fatal heart attack.[13]

In the years after his death, Jesse Owens has remained a public legend. His four gold medals, won under extraordinarily difficult world conditions, have assured him a lasting place in Olympic history. Today, even young Olympians who were not born when he died are awed when documentary footage of Jesse's heroics are shown on television.

In 1992, fifty-six years after Jesse's stunning performance in Berlin, *USA Today* conducted a survey of current Olympians to ask them to name the "greatest Summer Olympian of all time." The vote was a virtual split between Jesse Owens and Carl Lewis, the best-known American Olympic hero after 1980. Lewis received 22 percent of the vote to Owens's 19 percent, followed by swimmer Mark Spitz (11 percent) and discus thrower Al Oerter (6 percent).[14]

In Germany, officials paid tribute to Owens by giving a new name to the street outside Olympic Stadium, calling it Jesse Owens Strasse. Owens's name began appearing on a host of prestigious track awards, and Ohio State erected a beautiful track-and-field facility in his honor. Many of the awards included financial assistance for needy young people.

In the end, what might have mattered most about Jesse Owens's life was the example he set for youth of all races. In spite of great hardships, he persevered. When he faced his toughest battles, be they on the track or in his own mind, he gave his best effort.

In reviewing *Blackthink,* a *New York Times* writer may have unwittingly written the finest memorial that the runner could have wanted. "Jesse Owens," wrote Doc Young, "has had a thousand good reasons for giving up but never did."

In the end, only death could stop him. Owens once wrote the following about New York and San Francisco Giants star Willie Mays: "Every time he went back for a drive he couldn't possibly catch, and caught it, every time he doubled off the wall when they were throwing him low and outside in a clutch situation, every [black] kid in America—and a lot of white ones—knew for sure . . . that life was worth living and that this world was, all in all, a pretty good place. . . . He didn't have to tell any kids he cared about them. . . . He showed something more important—that he cared about *life,* and cared to the hilt. *That's* what they want to know—that a Negro can feel THAT."[15]

The same analogy can and must be made about Jesse Owens. When he ran and leaped, fans of every nation, religion and color responded to him. In spite of the primitive equipment and cinder-track surfaces of his day, he sprinted and soared like no one before him ever had done. He loved his sport and he loved his country and he loved mankind. Like Willie Mays, he made his fans feel life had value and that the world—though flawed—was something precious to enjoy each day.

In the final analysis, Jesse Owens—in spite of his human failings—merits admiration for his fight to improve relationships between the races as well as his significance as an athlete. During the last ten years of his life, he published two thoughtful books that gave the public his views on life, human relationships, and the pressing problems of the times.

In death, as in life, he attracted crowds. Many thousands of people attended his wake in the Arizona State

Capitol. Three days after he died, the man who had logged so many millions of miles in the air had one last flight. His body was taken to Chicago to lie in state at a local funeral parlor where many more people paid their respects. His burial in Chicago on April 4, 1980, brought two thousand people to the gravesite in spite of late snow.

An Olympic flag covered Jesse Owens's casket. His now-elderly college coach, Larry Snyder, stood by to give his star one last send-off, as did beloved Ruth, their children and grandchildren.[16]

Jesse Owens, the man who had come home to America in 1936 to be embraced by his country as a hero, was gone. All of his records had been broken. What remained was his remarkable story.

Through talent and determination, this grandson of freed slaves had overcome poverty and racism. A humble sharecropper's son, he had become an activist whose opinions and help had been sought by presidents and plain people alike. Like Martin Luther King, Jr., Owens too had his dreams.

Jesse Owens, the man, was dead.

Jesse Owens, the legend, lives on in all of us—black and white, brown and yellow, athlete and spectator.

Source Notes

Introduction

1. Jesse Owens and Paul Neimark, *The Jesse Owens Story* (New York: Putnam, 1970), 32, 39–41.
2. Ibid.

Chapter One

1. *The Jesse Owens Story*, p. 51.
2. William J. Baker, *Jesse Owens: An American Life* (New York: Free Press, 1988), pp. 5–10.
3. *The Jesse Owens Story*, p. 13.
4. Baker, p. 13.
5. Jesse Owens and Paul Neimark, *I Have Changed* (New York: Morrow, 1972), p. 90; Jesse Owens and Paul Neimark, *Blackthink: My Life As Black Man and White Man* (New York: Morrow, 1970), p. 25.
6. Nicholas Lemann, *The Promised Land: The Great Black Migration and How It Changed America* (New York: Knopf, 1991), pp. 7–8; Baker, p. 12.
7. *The Jesse Owens Story*, p. 13.
8. Jesse Owens and Paul Neimark, *Jesse: A Spiritual Autobiography* (Plainfield, N.J.: Logos International, 1978), p. 5.
9. *Jesse: A Spiritual Autobiography*, pp. 5–10.
10. Ibid., pp. 14–15.
11. Baker, p. 11.
12. *Jesse: A Spiritual Autobiography*, pp. 19–20.
13. Ibid., pp. 15–16.
14. Lemann, p. 6.

15. Ibid., p. 36.
16. *I Have Changed*, p. 67.
17. *Jesse: A Spiritual Autobiography*, p. 22.
18. Ibid., p. 22.

Chapter Two
 1. Baker, p. 18.
 2. Ibid., p. 26.
 3. Ibid., p. 19.
 4. *The Jesse Owens Story*, p. 26.
 5. Ibid., pp. 27–28.
 6. Kenneth L. (Tug) Wilson and Jerry Brondfield, *The Big Ten* (Englewood Cliffs, NJ: Prentice-Hall, 1967), p. 204.
 7. *The Jesse Owens Story*, p. 28.
 8. *Jesse: A Spiritual Biography*, p. 109.
 9. William O. Johnson, Jr., *All That Glitters Is Not Gold: The Olympic Game* (New York: Putnam, 1972), p. 66.
10. *Jesse: A Spiritual Biography*, p. 41; *The Jesse Owens Story*, p. 32; Baker, p. 23.
11. *The Jesse Owens Story*, p. 32.
12. *Jesse: A Spiritual Biography*, pp. 40–45.
13. Baker, 21.
14. Ibid., p. 22.
15. *The Jesse Owens Story*, p. 33.
16. Ibid., p. 32.
17. Ibid., p. 33.
18. Baker, p. 22.
19. Ibid., p. 24.

Chapter Three
 1. Lemann, p. 45.
 2. Ibid., p. 45; S. R. Spencer, Jr., "Booker T. Washington," in *The American Story* (edited by Earl Schenck Miers), pp. 251–252.
 3. Baker, p. 25.
 4. Ibid., p. 26; Johnson, p. 46.

5. Tony Gentry, *Jesse Owens* (New York: Chelsea House, 1990), p. 35.
6. Baker, pp. 26–28.
7. Ibid.
8. *Cleveland Gazette,* April 2, 1932; May 14, 1932; May 28, 1932.
9. Baker, p. 20.
10. *The Jesse Owens Story,* p. 36; Baker, pp. 19–20.
11. *I Have Changed,* pp. 81–83.
12. Baker, pp. 29–31.
13. *The Jesse Owens Story,* p. 36.
14. Gentry, p. 38.
15. Ibid.
16. Baker, p. 35.
17. Larry Snyder, "My Boy Jesse." *The Saturday Evening Post,* November 7, 1937, p. 14.
18. Ibid., p. 99.

Chapter Four
1. Baker, pp. 38–40.
2. *Blackthink,* p. 11; Baker, pp. 41, 47.
3. Johnson, p. 46.
4. Larry Snyder, "World's Greatest Athlete: How He Trains," *Scholastic Coach,* March 1936, p. 7.
5. *I Have Changed,* p. 31; Snyder, "World's Greatest Athlete," p. 32.
6. Snyder, "World's Greatest Athlete," p. 7; Snyder, *Post,* pp. 99–101; *Blackthink,* p. 22.
7. Snyder, "World's Greatest Athlete," p. 32.
8. Ibid.
9. Baker, p. 47.
10. *Blackthink,* pp. 11–13.
11. Ibid., p. 13.
12. *Blackthink,* pp. 15–16.
13. Baker, p. 55.
14. *The Jesse Owens Story,* p. 63.

15. Baker, pp. 55–56.
16. *Blackthink*, p. 17.

Chapter Five
1. Baker, p. 49, 67.
2. Snyder, *Post*, p. 14.
3. Grantland Rice, *The Tumult and the Shouting* (New York: Barnes, 1954), p. 253; *The New York Times*, August 28, 1956.
4. Baker, p. 51.
5. *The Jesse Owens Story*, p. 52.
6. *Chicago Tribune*, pp. 332–333.
7. Snyder, *Post*, p. 14.
8. Rice, p. 253.
9. *The Jesse Owens Story*, p. 58.
10. Rice, p. 253.
11. *Chicago Tribune*, p. 331.
12. Baker, p. 52.

Chapter Six
1. Baker, p. 57.
2. Ibid., pp. 57–58.
3. *Cleveland Call and Post*, August 22, 1935; *Cleveland Gazette*, July 27, 1935; *Cleveland Call and Post*, February 16, 1935; *Los Angeles Times*, July 10, 1935.
4. Baker, pp. 60–62.
5. John Hoberman, *The Olympic Crisis* (New Rochelle, NY: Aristide D. Caratzas, 1986), p. 104.
6. Baker, p. 45; James Michener, *Sports in America* (New York: Random House, 1976), p. 167.
7. Hoberman, p. 104, *Chicago Defender*, March 14, 1936; March 28, 1936.
8. Baker, pp. 65–66.
9. Ibid., pp. 62, 66.
10. Chris Mead, *Champion: Joe Louis, Black Hero in White America* (New York: Scribner, 1985), p. 103.

11. Ibid., p. 106.
12. Ibid., p. 87.
13. Ibid., pp. 99, 267.
14. *Jesse: A Spiritual Autobiography*, pp. 53–54.
15. *I Have Changed*, pp. 39–40.

Chapter Seven
1. Johnson, p. 51.
2. Unsigned Editorial, "Joe Louis and Jesse Owens, *The Crisis—A Record of the Darker Races*, August 1935, p. 241.
3. Mead, p. 103; *Jesse: A Spiritual Biography*, p. 61.
4. Ibid., p. 60.
5. *The Jesse Owens Story*, p. 74; Baker, p. 81.
6. *Chicago Tribune*, October 10, 1978.
7. Baker, p. 78.
8. Personal interview, Robert Waite, Ph.D.
9. John Toland, *Adolf Hitler*, volume 1 (Garden City, NY: Doubleday, 1976), p. 413.
10. Richard D. Mandell, *The Nazi Olympics* (Urbana: University of Illinois Press, 1987), p. xii.
11. Thomas Wolfe, *You Can't Go Home Again* (New York: Perennial Library Edition, 1973), p. 484.
12. Duff Hart-Davis, *Hitler's Games: The 1936 Olympics* (New York: Harper & Row, 1986), pp. 184-185.
13. Wolfe, p. 485; Baker, p. 93.
14. Mead, p. 103; Gordon A. Craig, *Germany: 1866–1945* (New York: Oxford, 1978), p. 632; Baker, p. 63
15. Snyder, *Post*, p. 97.
16. Ibid., pp. 14, 97; *The New York Times*, August 7, 1936; Hart-Davis, p. 163.
17. Snyder, *Post*, 97; Hart-Davis, p. 163.
18. Hart-Davis, p. 189.
19. Snyder, *Post*, 15.
20. Ibid., p. 15; Baker, pp. 83–84; Mead, p. 143.
21. *Jesse: A Spiritual Autobiography*, p. 62.

22. Ibid.

23. *The New York Times,* August 28, 1956.

24. Snyder, *Post,* p. 15.

Chapter Eight

1. Toland, p. 413.

2. Hart-Davis, p. 163.

3. Baker, pp. 91–92.

4. *I Have Changed,* p. 158.

5. Hart-Davis, p. 174.

6. David Chester, *The Olympic Games Handbook* (New York: Scribner, 1971), pp. 82–83.

7. Personal interview, Robert Waite.

8. Baker, p. 93.

9. Snyder, *Post,* p. 15.

10. Hart-Davis, pp. 175-176; *Post,* p. 100.

11. Hart-Davis, p. 163.

12. Baker, pp. 90–91.

13. Rice, p. 253.

Chapter Nine

1. Baker, pp. 94–95.

2. *The New York Times,* August 5, 1936.

3. Ibid.; *Jesse: A Spiritual Autobiography,* pp. 71–72.

4. Rice, p. 252.

5. *Jesse: A Spiritual Autobiography,* pp. 71–72; Baker, pp. 96–97.

6. *Jesse: A Spiritual Autobiography,* pp. 71–72.

7. Hart-Davis, pp. 128.

8. Ibid., p. 187.

9. Rice, p.252.

10. *I Have Changed,* p. 138; Gentry, p. 68.

11. Hart-Davis, p. 188.

12. Ibid.

13. *I Have Changed,* p. 134.

14. *The New York Times,* August 7, 1936; Baker, pp. 98, 100.

15. *Blackthink*, p. 156.
16. Baker, p. 99.
17. Gentry, p. 69.
18. Johnson, p. 179.
19. Ibid., p. 181.
20. Toland, p. 412.
21. Johnson, p. 180.
22. *The New York Times*, August 8, 1936; Baker, p. 104.
23. Johnson, p. 179.
24. Gentry, p. 73.
25. *The Jesse Owens Story*, pp. 64, 70.
26. Rice, p. 254.
27. Mead, p. 105; Rice p. 252.
28. Hoberman, p. 104.
29. Toland, p. 414.
30. Johnson, p. 145.

Chapter Ten
1. Snyder, *Post*, p. 97.
2. Ibid., p. 97; Baker, p. 110.
3. Snyder, *Post*, p. 98; Baker, p. 111.
4. *I Have Changed*, pp. 81–83; *Jesse*, pp. 111–112.
5. *I Have Changed*, pp. 81–83.
6. Snyder, *Post*, p. 97.
7. Ibid., pp. 98–101.
8. *Chicago Tribune*, August 18, 1936; *New York Times*, August 18, 1936.
9. Snyder, *Post*, pp. 98–100.
10. Ibid., pp. 98–101; *The New York Times*, August 18, 1936; Baker, 121.
11. Johnson, p. 44.
12. *The New York Times*, August 18, 1936; *New York Herald-Tribune*, August 25, 1936.
13. *Cleveland Call and Post*, August 27, 1936.
14. Baker, pp. 123–124.

15. "Saga of Jesse Owens," *The Crisis: A Record of the Darker Races*, September 1936, p. 267.
16. Ibid.
17. Snyder, *Post*, pp. 98–101.
18. *The Jesse Owens Story*, p. 84.
19. Johnson, pp. 48–49; *The Jesse Owens Story*, p. 84.
20. Gentry, p. 81; Johnson, p. 45.
21. Gentry, p. 83.
22. *Blackthink*, p. 37.
23. Ibid., p. 39; Gentry, 86.
24. *Blackthink*, p. 40.

Chapter Eleven
1. *I Have Changed*, pp. 85, 137.
2. Mead, p. 104.
3. Snyder, *Post*, p. 100.
4. Gentry, p. 88.
5. Johnson, p. 48.
6. Norman Katkov, "Jesse Owens, the Ebony Express," *Sport*, April 1954, p. 78.
7. *Blackthink*, p. 59.
8. *I Have Changed*, p. 19.
9. Ibid., p. 18.
10. Baker, pp. 165, 169.
11. *Blackthink*, p. 58.
12. Ibid., p. 59.
13. Mead, p. 225; Baker, p. 167.
14. Mead, p. 271.
15. Chester, p. 92.
16. Baker, p. 170.
17. *The New York Times*, August 28, 1956.
18. *Jesse Owens Returns to Berlin*, documentary film, ABC-TV, 1971.
19. Martin Bauml Duberman, *Paul Robeson* (New York: Knopf, 1988), pp. 527–528.

20. Ibid.
21. *The New York Times*, August 28, 1956, p. 24; Gentry, p. 96.
22. *The New York Times*, August 28, 1956.
23. "A Famous Athlete's Diplomatic Debut," *Life*, October 31, 1955, pp. 49–50.
24. *I Have Changed*, p. 90.
25. *The Jesse Owens Story*, p. 90.
26. Gentry, p. 97.

Chapter Twelve
1. Baker, p. 186.
2. *I Have Changed*, pp. 148–52.
3. Ibid., p. 153.
4. Baker, p. 189.
5. *I Have Changed*, p. 62.
6. Gentry, p. 97.
7. *Blackthink*, pp. 78–79.
8. Ibid., p. 145.
9. Ibid., pp. 137–40, 157.
10. Ibid., p. 111.
11. Ibid., p. 21; Baker, p. 205.
12. Johnson, p. 50.
13. *I Have Changed*, pp. 44–46.

Chapter Thirteen
1. *I Have Changed*, pp. 137–139.
2. Jesse Owens, "The Olympics: A Preview," *TV Guide*, October 12–18, 1978, pp. 6–10.
3. Johnson, p. 52.
4. Baker, pp. 207–10.
5. *Blackthink*, p. 64.
6. Ibid., pp. 35, 64.
7. Ibid., p. 88.
8. *The New York Times*, December 27, 1992; Wilson and Brondfield, p. 476.

9. Johnson, pp. 44, 52.
10. Ibid., p. 52.
11. *I Have Changed*, pp. 99–118; *The New York Times*, May 4, 1971.
12. Johnson, p. 41.
13. Baker, p. 220; Johnson, p. 45.
14. Johnson, p. 46.

Chapter Fourteen
1. *I Have Changed*, pp. 7–20, 72–80.
2. Ibid., pp. 91–92, 97, 100.
3. Ibid., pp. 9–10.
4. Ibid., p. 36.
5. Ibid., p. 41.
6. Ibid., pp. 140–141.

Chapter Fifteen
1. *I Have Changed*, p. 153.
2. *Blackthink*, p. 132.
3. *I Have Changed*, pp. 83–84.
4. Ibid., p. 84.
5. Ibid., p. 139.
6. Johnson, p. 47.
7. Baker, p. 219.
8. *I Have Changed*, p. 146.
9. *Chicago Tribune*, October 11, 1978.
10. Mead, pp. 286–287.
11. *Blackthink*, p. 113.
12. Baker, p. 225.
13. Mead, p. 287.
14. *USA Today*, July 22, 1992.
15. *Blackthink*, p. 134.
16. *Chicago Tribune*, April 5, 1980; *Washington Post*, April 5, 1980.

For Further Reading

Baker, William J. *Jesse Owens: An American Life.* New York: Free Press, 1988.

Butler, Octavia E. *Kindred.* Boston: Beacon Press, 1979.

Chester, David. *The Olympic Games Handbook.* New York: Scribner, 1971.

Craig, Gordon A. *Germany: 1866–1945.* New York: Oxford, 1978.

Duberman, Martin Bauml. *Paul Robeson.* New York: Knopf, 1988.

Gentry, Tony. *Jesse Owens.* New York: Chelsea House Publishers, 1990.

Hart-Davis, Duff. *Hitler's Games.* New York: Harper & Row, 1986.

Hoberman, John. *The Olympic Crisis.* New Rochelle, NY: Aristide D. Caratzas, 1986.

Johnson, William O. *All That Glitters Is Not Gold.* New York: Putnam, 1972.

Katkov, Norman. "Jesse Owens: The Ebony Express," *Sport,* April 1954.

Lemann, Nicholas. *The Promised Land.* New York: Knopf, 1991.

Mandell, Richard D. *The Nazi Olympics.* Urbana: University of Illinois Press, 1987.

Mead, Chris. *Champion: Joe Louis, Black Hero in White America.* New York: Scribner, 1985.

Michener, James. *Sports in America.* New York: Random House, 1976.

Moore, Kenny. "A Courageous Stand," *Sports Illustrated,* August 5, 1991.

Nuwer, Hank. *Sports Scandals.* New York: Franklin Watts, 1995.

Owens, Jesse, and Paul Neimark. *Blackthink: My Life as Black Man and White Man.* New York: Pocket Books, 1971.

——. *I Have Changed.* New York: Morrow, 1972.

——. *Jesse: A Spiritual Autobiography.* Plainfield, NJ: Logos International, 1978.

——. *The Jesse Owens Story.* New York: Putnam, 1970.

Owens, Jesse. "The Olympics: A Preview," *TV Guide*, October 12–18, 1978.

Rice, Grantland. *The Tumult and the Shouting.* New York: Barnes, 1954.

Sabin, Francene. *Jesse Owens: Olympic Hero.* New York: Troll, 1990.

Snyder, Larry. "My Boy Jesse," *The Saturday Evening Post,* November 7, 1937.

——. "World's Greatest Athlete: How He Trains," *Scholastic Coach*, March 1936.

Spencer, S. R. "Booker T. Washington," in *The American Story* (edited by Earl Schenck Miers). Great Neck, NY: Channel Press, 1956.

Toland, John. *Adolf Hitler*, volume 1. Garden City, NY: Doubleday, 1976.

Tuite, James. *Sports of The Times: The Arthur Daley Years.* New York: New York Times Book Company, 1975.

Tygiel, Jules. *Baseball's Great Experiment.* New York: Oxford, 1983.

Unsigned Article. "A Famous Athlete's Diplomatic Debut." *Life*, October 31, 1955.

Unsigned Editorial. "Joe Louis and Jesse Owens," *The Crisis: A Record of the Darker Races*, August 1935.

Unsigned Article. "Saga of Jesse Owens," *The Crisis: A Record of the Darker Races*, September 1936.

Wilson, Kenneth L., and Jerry Brondfield. *The Big Ten.* Englewood Cliffs, NJ: Prentice-Hall, 1967.

Internet Sites

Jesse Owens
http://www.cmgww.com/sports/owens/owens.html
Sponsored by CMG Worldwide and offering career highlights, a photo gallery, and quotes about Owens.

Jesse Owens Foundation
http://www.jesse-owens.org
Offers a biography of Owens and information about the foundation.

Track & Field Online
http://www.trackonline.com
Features articles about track and field athletes, supplements and nutrition, and interviews.

USA Track and Field
http://www.usatf.org
Features current athletes, meet results, and information on membership.

Index

172

About the Author

Hank Nuwer is the author of *Steroids, Recruiting in Sports, Sports Scandals,* and other books for Franklin Watts. He is completing two more Franklin Watts titles, *To the Young Athlete* and *To the Young Writer,* as well as *Wrongs of Passage,* a book for Indiana University Press on the societal problems of hazing and binge drinking.

He received undergraduate and graduate degrees in English respectively from Buffalo State College and New Mexico Highlands University. He has interviewed hundreds of sports personalities such as Carl Lewis, Al Oerter, Joe Paterno, and Bobby Bowden. He served as consultant on the NBC-TV movie *Moment of Truth: Broken Pledges,* based on *Broken Pledges,* his book about hazing deaths in colleges. The movie starred major league baseball player Barry Bonds. On assignment for magazines, Nuwer played first base for the now-disbanded Indianapolis Clowns and for a Montreal Expos minor league team managed by Felipe Alou.

Married to editor Jenine Howard Nuwer, he has two sons, Adam and Christian.